100 BOLD RECIPES FOR A MOSTLY HEALTHY LIFESTYLE

PLANT ⟶ FORWARD

JAZMIN & RICHARD BLAIS

VICTORY BELT PUBLISHING INC.

LAS VEGAS

First published in 2023 by Victory Belt Publishing Inc.

ISBN-13: 978-1-628601-35-0

The author is not a licensed practitioner, physician, or medical professional and offers no medical diagnoses, treatments, suggestions, or counseling. The information presented herein has not been evaluated by the U.S. Food and Drug Administration, and it is not intended to diagnose, treat, cure, or prevent any disease. Full medical clearance from a licensed physician should be obtained before beginning or modifying any diet, exercise, or lifestyle program, and physicians should be informed of all nutritional changes.

The author/owner claims no responsibility to any person or entity for any liability, loss, or damage caused or alleged to be caused directly or indirectly as a result of the use, application, or interpretation of the information presented herein.

Cover photo and design, interior design, and illustrations by Justin-Aaron Velasco and Kat Lannom

Lifestyle photos by Christopher Regan

Recipe photos by Dani McReynolds

Printed in Canada

TC 0123

To Our Family, Friends, and Supporters

CONTENTS

INTRODUCTION

Here we go. My third cookbook. Truth be told, there's no way I would have thought fifteen years ago that I'd be publishing a single book, much less three. When I was a young chef, there was *Joy of Cooking,* and then cookbooks from specific restaurants and chefs started to hit the scene. Cookbooks by chefs who ran prestigious restaurants were gold in those pre-internet days. They gave us a bird's-eye view inside renowned kitchens, a peek behind the curtain of haute cuisine, and we gobbled up every page. This makes me sound old, and that too may be the truth, but it's an essential part of my story.

Cookbooks can be everlasting and tangible art, and as a fan of so many chefs and cookbooks alike, I've assembled a nice little library. Now, with interest in restaurants, food, and cooking being even more widespread, there are many types of cookbooks. Back then, I could only dream of dining in the world's top restaurants because of the travel and expense it would involve. However, thumbing through the Charlie Trotter series gave me a glimpse into a kitchen and world I so wanted to be a part of. These cookbooks taught me about so many ingredients I had never touched, worked with, or even seen. Some of these cookbooks, like Marco Pierre White's classic *White Heat,* were like rock records that any serious, aspiring young cook worth their salt would own.

There are more to mention, of course, and some of the books in my collection feature chefs I've come to know and admire, both before and since I've worked with or appeared on-screen with them, like Gordon Ramsay, Tom Colicchio, and Eric Ripert. Another classic, *The French Laundry Cookbook,* comes to mind; this book was created while I was working at the French Laundry under Thomas Keller. It was the first time some of these recipes were released to the world. It both validated my time there and acted as a physical placeholder for the arc of my career; it also, in the age before the internet, helped me consolidate all of the recipes I'd dutifully scribbled out in Moleskines and on note cards. Everybody traded recipes in those days, and safeguarding your treasured collection was paramount.

These "best of the restaurant" types of cookbooks made the cataloging and sharing of recipes much easier. Books like these were, for lack of a better word, bibles to young cooks like me. They were passed along and borrowed, with worn covers and well-thumbed pages. This book is *not* one of those books.

And then there is a class of cookbook that always, well, kind of bothered me. And I mean this in the most respectful way. I'm talking about the sort of book that sits on the shelf of a fancy home accoutrement store. The book that has a slice of avocado toast on its cover and is chock-full of colorful vegetables, its pages littered with sheet pan dishes and easy-to-make one-pot meals. These books irked me because, well, they are so delicious looking. You may not have heard of the authors, or the author may be a celebrity from your favorite TV show as a kid, but the food and the artistry made me want to kick myself. These books are bestsellers sometimes! Lifestyle cookbooks, if you will, filled with recipes that seem and are for the most part easy. You can be Martha Stewart or Gwyneth Paltrow too! You can make hummus as well as they do in the Middle East for your kids' healthy lunches!

If I'm being honest, these books bothered me because I was jealous. If it's so carefree and easy, why wasn't I writing those books? After I grew more comfortable as a chef and artist and human, I created a book that comes close, and I continually create and share recipes in this category, for it's a genre of recipe writing that encompasses most of food media. Now, I'm not bothered at all by these books—quite the opposite, I'm inspired by them. But this book is not one of those cookbooks, either.

Another common type of cookbook is the self-help, nutrition, diet, better for you, do this, lose weight, only eat this, type. And I have to be honest, I don't own any of these books, although my wife, Jazmin, owns tons. I've never been one to admit I need help, but if you've seen me play golf or followed along the swerving journey that is my hairstyle or, god forbid, my parenting, then you might suggest that help, guidance, a few tips might be useful. Yet, after fifty years of life, sometimes grumpily plodding along, sometimes angsty and pretentious, sometimes lost as a dreamer who thinks he knows better, I've come to understand that we all need help sometimes. We live in a world where help is a click—or, in this case, a book—away. *That* is what this book is about.

FOOD THAT LOOKS GOOD

FINE DINING FOR KIDS

HOW TO EAT THIS WAY

HOW TO EAT THAT WAY

HOW CAN I HELP?

How can I help: a four-word sentence that can make anyone a better person. I used to end every pre-shift meeting at my restaurants with the phrase "Questions, comments, concerns?" But what I was really asking was "How can I help? How can I share my knowledge in this arena to help you advance and succeed?" I'm in the position of having a skill that can help people because we all eat. But we don't all eat well. Given the choice between subsisting on fast food and eating food that makes us strong and healthy and helps us live our best life, we're taking the latter option if all other variables are equal. If it cost the same, tasted great, and could be ready in the same amount of time, we'd all pick the one that helps, not hurts. Wouldn't we? I know I didn't for many years. I cooked inspired food in restaurants where people waited months for a reservation, and then I'd eat greasy fast food for dinner. I worked with some of the best ingredients in the world and drank diet soda and light beer. Sometimes even when we know better, we don't do better. But this was almost two decades ago, and in that time, I've learned and grown a lot, especially when it comes to healthful choices.

Ever heard the phrase "Abs are made in the kitchen"? It's cute, and I've never made abs happen for me personally, but I subscribe to the theory. What you eat either powers you or drains you. I know because I've lived it myself. We are in control of what we eat, so why not learn to cook better food? Eat good *and* healthy food is a mantra for me in my own life. This doesn't mean that every once in a while on a road trip, I'm not pulling off to get a Whopper, but it's incredibly rare and balanced by the healthy food I eat the other 95 percent of the time. In fact, I can tell you exactly when I last ate a Whopper; it was in July 2020 on the way to Zion National Park. It was delicious.

So, back to the question of how I can help. I'm a chef, and I know how to make food taste delicious. It's a superpower, I guess, and although it's not as amazing as the ability to fly, it's incredibly useful. In this book, I plan to pass my superpower on to you in parts, giving you the ability to add well-seasoned, thoughtfully created, nourishing recipes to your repertoire.

This isn't a health food book. This is a *healthier* cookbook. What's the difference, you ask? I think some of it is in the approach. I'm starting with tried-and-true, delicious food and making healthier choices within each recipe that won't upend the entire dish. Have you ever made a recipe that claimed to be a healthy version of a dish only to end up with something totally different—not bad or worse, just different? I don't want that here. I can't pretend that a slice of sweet potato is toast no matter how hard I try. I want pizza to look and taste like pizza. I want people to gasp when you tell them the pumpkin bread is gluten free or the tuna salad has no tuna in it. This book is for people who LOVE food *and* want to eat a bit healthier. Yes, you can do both!

OK, you've read this far into the intro, which most people skip, to be honest, and now you might be wondering...

WHY SHOULD YOU LISTEN TO ME?

Well, if you have followed the journey of my career at all, you know I've been through transitions of hair, weight, and style as well as food during my television exploits of the last fifteen years. You may know that I've lost sixty-plus pounds, run seven marathons, cut out alcohol, and maintained a healthy lifestyle all while opening dozens of restaurants and eating or cooking on television regularly.

Here is where I risk it all for the price of honesty: there isn't *one* special formula, fitness regimen, or nutrition plan that helped me do it. I'm not going to tell you how to lose weight because everyone's journey is different, and weight loss might not even be a goal for you. It was one of mine early on, but now I'm more interested in living a life that makes me feel good and powerful. I'm not going to tell you to *only* eat certain things because everyone's life and health are different. And I'm certainly not going to tell you what cardio you should do or that a combination of marathon training, yoga, SoulCycle, and a golf obsession is the secret recipe. Fitness, especially, is personal. But I will tell you what helped me get healthier, which is all of the above, plus...

The plus, for me, was Jazmin Blais. I joke that I had to *run* after her to get her to marry me, and it's kind of true. We met well before I ever appeared in front of a camera or on your television. We met when I was at my most unhealthy, mentally, physically, and even emotionally. I had just closed my first namesake restaurant—or, more accurately, it had failed epically, and the investors closed it on me. I mention Jazmin here not because it's sweet but because it's true. She was my first "why." I've had other "whys" since, but she was the first reason why I wanted to get healthy, plus she gave me the beginnings of the "how" for my body.

Jazmin has acted as a coach and a guru for me and others. She was a personal trainer throughout college and went on to get her master's degree in public health from Emory University. She's also a trained yoga instructor and mindfulness-based stress reduction practitioner. When we married, she took a break from the health field and helped me open and run restaurants. She wrote menus, trained staff, and ran the financials. She's a whiz, truly. She takes all of these modalities and combines them to create a better wellness outlook for our family and beyond. And she is the coach and guru of this book, our first truly co-authored work.*

I bring up Jazmin as the plus because you can cook all of the recipes in this book, even double down nutritionally and physically, and still not make the gains or achieve the goals you want if you don't have a reason to commit to your health. You need a "why." You need a catalyst, an emotional crossroads. The prospect of love and a future together was my catalyst. What's yours?

*In many households, especially ones that involve TV celebrities, there is the person who gets all of the attention and the person behind the scenes who gets things done. Ours is kind of like this, so I do a lot of the talking in this book, even though Jazmin was my equal partner in creating it.

Of course, this is a cookbook, one with *Plant* in the title, so you may have picked up on the obvious theme. Most of these recipes are plant focused—not fully plant based or vegetarian, but eschewing the old-school American formula of a "dish" having a large chunk of protein at the center. These recipes are also incredibly mindful of how much and what kind of sugar is used. More and more research shows that we humans are eating way too much refined sugar and processed food. If you've never thought about swapping out white sugar for better alternatives, this book gives you some tips on how to do it wisely without compromising flavor. These recipes are attentive to how much and what kind of flour is used, and the same goes for dairy. They are mindful of dairy and soy alternatives. And they are mindful of limiting deep-fried foods and swapping in healthier oils.

Mindful is the keyword here. We feel that every recipe is healthy; indeed, this is the type of nourishing food we eat at home with our kids. *Healthy* has become a buzzword in food, though, one that can morph and change and mean many different things to many different people. What's healthy for one person may be unhealthy for others. Nowhere is this more true than in what we put in our bodies. Food sensitivities, allergies, and autoimmune issues can turn a simple ingredient used by many into an unhealthy choice for you. It's good to know about these proclivities and speak with a doctor if you have any issues that impact what you can eat.

Generally, though, the tenets of how we define *healthy* in our life and in this cookbook are as follows:

- Remove refined sugars (such as granulated white sugar and corn syrup) and processed sugar alternatives (including sucralose and aspartame).

- Limit gluten, flour, and simple carbohydrates.

- Replace dairy with lactose-free or dairy-free options.

- Limit processed foods and oils.

- Enjoy plant-forward meals regularly.

Staying within these guidelines has helped me lose weight and keep it off. Equally important to me is that I enjoy cooking this type of food, and I enjoy eating it too! Here's something that surprises a lot of people who know I'm a chef: I like oat milk and cauliflower pizza crust. I like cashew cheese, kefir, and coconut sugar. I may actually prefer these things to their more traditional counterparts. I'm a chef, some say one of the most creative in all the land (OK, I'm the only one who says that), and I love the creativity of these alternatives. I like that they can be used in a myriad of ways, and I like how they make me think outside the box to balance flavors and textures.

> "YOU DON'T HAVE TO LIKE IT, BUT YOU DO HAVE TO TRY IT"

As Jazmin and I tell our kids, you don't have to like it, but you do have to try it. Even when our teenager says no, she's saying it less often than she did as a toddler, so you've gotta appreciate the mantra. That mantra is a lifestyle in and of itself. Can you live it? You might love it, both how it tastes and how it makes you feel.

WHERE TO GO FROM HERE

A "why" helps. A mantra helps. A resource helps. Your why and your mantra are personal, and they are yours to dictate. The resource is this book. We have organized this book by ingredient so you could easily find a few inspirational recipes for a favorite vegetable. And maybe you'll find that if you really love Bolognese, shakshouka is your next dish to try and expand your repertoire of plant-focused meals. Alternatively, if you don't think you like greens, maybe a recipe in the greens chapter will entice you to try something new. Cooking and eating your way through this book will help you expand the limits of what healthy food can be.

Another resource I'll leave you with is my own personal cheat sheet gleaned from the last few decades of my health journey. Start with phase 1 and see what changes you notice as you progress. In some ways, the phases get easier as you go because you are actively making better choices on your own. Good luck and good health!

BLAIS CHEAT SHEET

PHASE 1:

1. I STOPPED DRINKING ALCOHOL.
2. I ADOPTED CASUAL FITNESS, RUNNING 2 TO 5 MILES A WEEK, AND SET A DAILY STEP GOAL (10,000).
3. I STOPPED DRINKING SODA AND SUGARY JUICES. LITTLE TO NO EMPTY-CALORIE LIQUIDS.
4. I REMOVED FAST FOOD ENTIRELY.

PHASE 2:

1. I STARTED MONITORING LATE-NIGHT EATING. JAZMIN STOPS EATING MOST DAYS BY 6PM. I'M MORE OF AN 8PM GUY. FIND THE CUTOFF THAT WORKS FOR YOU AND STICK TO IT. A LOT OF TIMES SNACKING IS HABITUAL, NOT SOMETHING YOUR BODY ACTUALLY CRAVES.
2. I LIMITED DESSERTS TO SPECIAL OCCASIONS. I'VE ACTUALLY BECOME MORE OF A SWEETS GUY AS I'VE GOTTEN OLDER, SO THIS IS ONE I STILL KEEP A CHECK ON.
3. I BEGAN RUNNING TWO OR THREE TIMES PER WEEK AND ADDED IN WEIGHT TRAINING TWICE A WEEK.

PHASE 3:

1. STILL NO ALCOHOL.
2. I IMPLEMENTED INTERMITTENT FASTING. I HAVE A NINE-HOUR WINDOW DURING WHICH I EAT MY MEALS. I STOP EATING BY 7PM MOST NIGHTS AND HAVE BREAKFAST AT AROUND 11AM THE NEXT DAY.

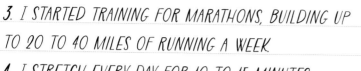

3. I STARTED TRAINING FOR MARATHONS, BUILDING UP TO 20 TO 40 MILES OF RUNNING A WEEK.

4. I STRETCH EVERY DAY FOR 10 TO 15 MINUTES.

5. I LIMIT FAST FOOD TO A FEW TIMES A YEAR—ADMITTEDLY PAINFUL FOR A KID WHOSE FIRST JOB WAS AT MCDONALD'S.

6. A FEW TIMES A YEAR, I REMOVE SUGAR, FLOUR, DAIRY, SOY, AND ANYTHING FRIED FOR SIX WEEKS. IT'S A HEALTH CHECK-IN THAT RESETS MY PALATE, WHICH I LOVE. IT'S AMAZING HOW SWEET EVEN SOMETHING LIKE KETCHUP TASTES AFTER ONE OF THESE CLEANSES.

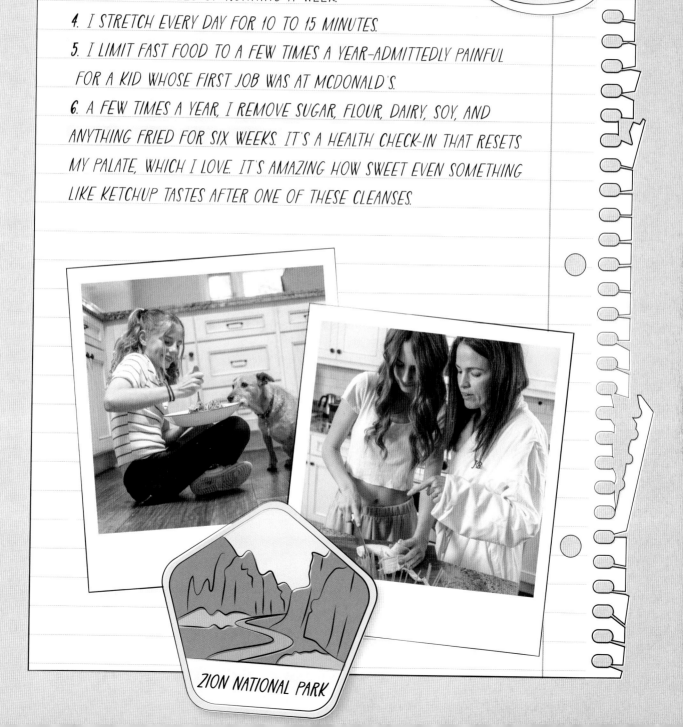

ZION NATIONAL PARK

INGREDIENTS WE LEAN ON

INGREDIENT	REPLACES	BENEFITS/WHY
Avocado oil mayonnaise	Mayonnaise or aioli	Avocado oil mayonnaise is a great substitute for traditional mayo, which has very little nutritional value (but is delicious). Swapping out the canola, soybean, or vegetable oil found in many mayonnaises for avocado oil ups the nutritional content and swaps the polyunsaturated fats for monounsaturated fats. Monounsaturated fats are generally regarded as a healthier option and are a vital part of the Mediterranean diet. There are even many vegan versions of avocado oil mayo, omitting the eggs.
Coconut aminos	Soy sauce and tamari	Coconut aminos is made from the fermented sap of the coconut palm tree. Despite the name, it doesn't have a coconut flavor; the taste is similar to soy sauce but less salty. It also adds umami to a dish just like soy sauce.
Coconut sugar	Granulated sugar and brown sugar	Coconut sugar is made from the sap of the coconut palm tree. It has been found to be lower on the glycemic index than traditional white sugar, which means it will not raise the body's blood sugar levels as quickly. It also contains inulin, a type of fiber that has been shown to slow glucose absorption in the body.
Ghee	Whole butter and/or oil	Ghee is butter that has been heated to remove the milk solids, leaving just the liquid fats. The milk solids in butter will burn if left on the heat for an extended period of time, which makes ghee a great choice when searing or cooking at higher heats. Ghee is anti-inflammatory and easier to digest than oils and butter for some people.
Kefir	Yogurt, sour cream, mayonnaise, and applesauce (in baking recipes)	Kefir is a tart, cultured, fermented milk drink with a thinner consistency than yogurt. It is a great source of calcium and protein and has probiotics for better gut health. Some people with lactose intolerance can tolerate kefir. Fermented foods have been shown to ease inflammation and improve gut health.
Miso	Umami flavor provided by meat	Miso is a fermented soybean product that is rich in probiotics. It contains many healthy vitamins and minerals, protein, and calcium. It is helpful for gut health and immune function. We use the paste version to flavor sauces and soups and as a marinade. It's the same miso used as a base for the miso soup you get at your corner sushi restaurant.
Nutritional yeast	Cheese	Nutritional yeast is a deactivated form of brewer's yeast. It's a good source of protein and vitamin B12, especially for vegetarians who have a hard time getting those two staples. It's a stellar substitute for cheese if you're trying to eat dairy free and is good sprinkled on popcorn. It also adds umami to vegetarian and vegan dishes.
Stevia	Table sugar, granulated sugar, and powdered sugar	Stevia is a popular low-glycemic, no-calorie sweetener derived from the plant of the same name. It is intensely sweet, sometimes as much as 300 times sweeter than table sugar, while not raising the body's blood sugar levels. It is also stable at higher temperatures so can be used in baking (unlike some other no-calorie sweeteners).

GRIBICHE

BLUEBERRY CHIA JAM

VEGETARIAN DEMI GLACE

RICHIE'S RANCH

BALSAMIC GLAZE

CASHEW CHEESE

ESCABECHE

MISO MUSTARD

PANTRY

I once had a restaurant in Atlanta called The Spence. *Spence* is an old English word for *pantry*, and I tell you this to inform you that I love a well-stocked pantry enough to name a restaurant after it. Condiments, sauces, dressings, and the like are sometimes the easiest way to eat a little healthier. We are playing the marginal gains game here.

One thing that differentiates healthy food from tasty healthy food is a good sauce that adds acid, bite, and vigor. Yes, you can buy sauces from a store, but they are usually chock-full of sugar, sodium, and preservatives. I grew up eating that green-topped ranch dressing too, but when you make your own ranch dressing, not only will you be adding a superfood to your diet instantly (i.e., kefir), but you'll feel superhuman. You will experience the thrill that comes along with saying you made the dressing, the salsa, the sauce. It's empowering for any cook and a big next-level step in cooking at home.

We put this chapter in the book to give you easy access to some of these instant upgrades. Even if you buy a rotisserie chicken at the store, you can still whip up a chunky chimichurri to complement it and watch your family gobble it up. These pantry staples amplify many of the dishes in this book, and we always give you the recipe name and page number so you can find them easily.

RICHIE'S RANCH DRESSING

OPTION

Every time we are in the throes of opening a restaurant, I threaten to name the restaurant Richie's, to the chagrin of my business partners and wife. I'll put it in writing right here, though, that the first restaurant I name Richie's is most certainly going to serve this tasty version of ranch dressing. We've glammed it up by replacing some of the heavier and more caloric ingredients with kefir and a healthy mayo option (we like Chosen Foods brand). If you've never tried kefir, a fermented yogurt drink, this is definitely the place to do it! Adding a serving of fermented foods to your daily diet is great for your digestive system too. Use this dressing on salads or as a dip for baked wings or even serve it with your pizza!

1 sun-dried tomato

2 tablespoons bacon drippings (optional but highly recommended; see Notes)

½ cup plain kefir

½ cup avocado oil mayonnaise

1 teaspoon red wine vinegar or sherry vinegar (use 2 teaspoons if using bacon drippings)

1 teaspoon dried dill weed

½ teaspoon dried chives

½ teaspoon dried parsley

½ teaspoon garlic powder

½ teaspoon onion powder

Juice of ½ lemon

Splash of coconut aminos (optional; see Notes)

Pinch of salt

Grind or two of black pepper

Hydrate the sun-dried tomato in warm water while you gather and measure all of the other ingredients.

Heat the bacon drippings, if using, until liquidy. Drain the sun-dried tomato and roughly chop it.

Place everything in a blender (or use a wide-mouth pint-sized jar and an immersion blender) and blend until smooth. This dressing should have a paintlike consistency. If it's too thick, add a bit of water and blend again. Taste and adjust with additional salt and/or pepper, if needed.

Store in an airtight container in the refrigerator for up to a week.

NOTES

The bacon drippings add some smoky, meaty flavor notes that make for a more complex ranch dressing. Omit them to make the dressing vegetarian.

The coconut aminos replaces the drip of soy sauce I normally would add to a dressing. It ups the umami quotient and the complexity!

GARLIC & MINT YOGURT SAUCE

Commonly known as tzatziki, this Mediterranean-inspired yogurt sauce will find a home on many recipes. The brightness of the cucumber and yogurt balances grilled meats, and the mint and garlic add a great "cheffy" nuance to this dip.

USED IN: Zucchini al Pastor (page 164), Baked Falafel (page 270)

½ cup plain Greek yogurt

1 teaspoon granulated garlic, or 1 clove garlic, grated

½ teaspoon dried mint

1 small Persian cucumber, finely diced

Juice of 1 lemon wedge

Pinch of salt

Pinch of freshly ground black pepper

Put all of the ingredients in a small mixing bowl and whisk until well combined. Store in an airtight container in the refrigerator for up to a week.

MY FAVORITE EGG DRESSING
(SAUCE GRIBICHE)

The title says it all, but maybe not in the best way. What even is egg dressing? Its actual name is gribiche, and it's a classic sauce. The mysterious intertwining of the licorice scent of the tarragon and the creaminess of the eggs works perfectly against the salty-sweet burst of the relish and capers. My favorite way to use this is over some gently steamed asparagus, but it would take to lots of other vegetables as well as seared steak or salmon.

2 large eggs, hard-boiled, peeled, and finely chopped

¼ cup extra-virgin olive oil

¼ cup chopped fresh parsley

1 tablespoon chopped fresh tarragon

Grated zest and juice of 1 lemon

1 tablespoon sherry vinegar

1½ teaspoons sweet pickle relish

1½ teaspoons Dijon mustard

2 teaspoons capers, drained

¼ teaspoon salt, plus more if desired

A few grinds of black pepper

Dash of Tabasco sauce

Put all of the ingredients in a small mixing bowl and whisk until well combined. Store in an airtight container in the refrigerator for up to a week.

NOTE

My perfect hard-boiled egg is cooked in boiling water for 13 minutes and then shocked in ice water.

BLAIS BÉARNAISE

I swear not all of these pantry recipes will be a play on our name, but here we are nonetheless. Who doesn't love a good béarnaise sauce? It's a creamy, rich sauce that's traditionally served with a nice steak. I'm not going to alter too much here because I think béarnaise is perfect, but I do save the extra work and use whole butter instead of clarified butter. I also recommend drizzling this sauce over some roasted vegetables or an eggplant or cauliflower steak (see page 90). Béarnaise is best used immediately, but leftover sauce will hold in the fridge for a few days, and you can gently warm it in a small saucepan, whisking it to bring it back to a nice texture. I've also been known to scoop refrigerated béarnaise like cold butter and place on top of a ribeye with zero shame.

¼ cup (½ stick) unsalted butter

¼ cup finely diced white onions

¼ cup champagne vinegar or distilled white vinegar

1 tablespoon freshly ground black pepper

½ teaspoon dried tarragon

1 large egg yolk

1 lemon wedge

1 teaspoon salt

Melt the butter in a microwave-safe bowl in the microwave. Set aside to cool.

Put the onions, vinegar, pepper, and tarragon in a small saucepan over medium heat. Bring to a boil, then lower the heat to maintain a simmer and cook until about 1 tablespoon of liquid remains, 3 to 5 minutes. Set aside to cool.

Set up a double boiler by placing a small heatproof glass bowl over another small saucepan with a few inches of water in it, making sure the water isn't touching the bottom of the bowl. Bring the water to a rolling boil.

Put the egg yolk in the glass bowl over the boiling water and whisk continuously for 30 seconds. Slowly drizzle in the melted butter while whisking continuously until the mixture thickens to a mayonnaise consistency. Strain the vinegar/tarragon reduction, then stir it into the egg mixture. Turn off the heat and pull the bowl off the saucepan.

Finish with a squeeze of lemon and the salt. Use immediately.

MISO MUSTARD

Miso is an amazing ingredient to start using if you don't use it already. It's an automatic upgrade, infusing just about any dish with a complex but approachable umami flavor hit. Miso is a fermented food that brings beneficial enzymes, B vitamins, omega-3 fatty acids, and healthy gut flora to your digestive system. This condiment became a staple in our house because of its variety of uses. Spread it over a grilled salmon fillet or toss it with some roasted Brussels sprouts—the choices are endless.

½ cup drippings from a roast (see Notes)

2 tablespoons white miso

2 tablespoons prepared yellow mustard (see Notes)

1 tablespoon water

Salt to taste

Warm the drippings in a small saucepan over medium-low heat. Remove the pan from the heat and whisk in the remaining ingredients until fully incorporated. Store in an airtight container in the refrigerator for up to a week.

NOTES

Pan drippings from a roast are my preferred base, but if you don't have that, chicken stock will work in a pinch; if using chicken stock, omit the tablespoon of water. You could even use the rendered fat and juices from the bottom of a rotisserie chicken bag.

I prefer French's mustard because it has no added sugar.

QUICK PICKLES

There are a few things that can make any home cook feel like a chef…even if it's just a chef on TikTok. One of those things, in my mind, is making homemade pickles. It's retro, it's cool, it's trend-worthy! This recipe can be doubled, tripled, quadrupled to your heart's content. You can also swap in other veggies to see what you like best. Everything is a pickle if you try hard enough.

USED IN: **The 50/50 Mushroom Burger (page 216)**

1 medium slicing cucumber

2 teaspoons salt

3 tablespoons distilled white vinegar

2 tablespoons agave nectar

1 teaspoon coriander seeds, cracked

1 teaspoon dill seeds

1 whole clove

½ teaspoon freshly ground black pepper

Wash the cucumber and pat dry. Slice into ¼-inch coins, place in a shallow bowl, and sprinkle with the salt. Set aside for 1 hour.

During that time, mix the remaining ingredients in a 12-ounce mason jar, shaking to incorporate.

Transfer the cucumber slices to a colander and rinse with cold water. Add the cucumber to the jar and shake to cover all of the slices in the brine. They'll be pickles in less than an hour but get better as they sit. Store in the refrigerator for up to 2 weeks.

CHIMICHURRI

This pantry staple is all about texture. You decide how much or how little to blend it. I prefer it barely processed and super chunky, while Jazmin likes it a little more homogeneous and blended. With its bold flavor, a little goes a long way here. Spread this sauce over Potatostones (page 108) or the vegetable of your choice. It would also work well on a piece of fish, some sliced rotisserie chicken, or a grilled cauliflower steak. We love to have a jar of this in the fridge for most any meal.

2 cups fresh flat-leaf parsley sprigs

½ cup fresh dill (fronds and some tender stems)

½ cup fresh tarragon leaves

¼ cup extra-virgin olive oil, or more as needed

¼ small white onion, chopped

2 teaspoons capers, drained

1 teaspoon anchovy paste

2 cloves garlic, roughly chopped

½ teaspoon salt

½ teaspoon freshly ground black pepper

Juice of 1 lemon

Place all of the ingredients in a food processor and process to the desired consistency. If you want a very smooth sauce, you may need to increase the amount of oil. Store in a tightly sealed jar in the refrigerator for up to a week.

ESCABECHE
(SPICY PICKLED CARROTS)

I'd never experienced taco shops—like, real taco shops—until we moved to Southern California. I love everything about your local corner spot, food truck, or pop-up taco stand. You really can't go wrong popping into any taco shop in a strip mall in California. It's going to be amazing. And one thing I can never resist is that baggie of spicy pickled carrots to go with my order. This recipe aspires to be just as good and offers a piquant little bite to any meal or taco. You don't have to store them in plastic baggies, but it would be cool if you did.

1 cup distilled white vinegar

1 cup apple cider vinegar

1 cup water

2 teaspoons salt

3 large carrots, sliced into 1-inch-thick coins

2 large jalapeño peppers, sliced into rings

½ cup cherry tomatoes, halved

½ small white onion, sliced

4 cloves garlic, peeled

3 bay leaves

2 teaspoons dried Mexican oregano

1 teaspoon black peppercorns

1 teaspoon chopped fresh basil

1 teaspoon chopped fresh cilantro

Bring the vinegars, water, and salt to a boil in a medium-sized saucepan; continue boiling until the salt is fully dissolved. Add the carrots, lower the heat to maintain a simmer, and cook for 3 minutes. Add the jalapeños, tomatoes, onion, garlic, bay leaves, oregano, and peppercorns and simmer for another 5 to 7 minutes, until the jalapeños are a dull green (the carrots should still be rather firm).

Remove the pan from the heat and stir in the herbs. Allow to cool before using; they can be eaten as soon as they've cooled to room temperature but taste even better after sitting overnight or for at least 8 hours. Store in airtight glass jars with enough of the pickling liquid to cover the carrots and jalapeños. They will keep for up to 2 weeks in the refrigerator.

WILD BLUEBERRY CHIA JAM

The magic of this jam is that it's made without pectin and still sets. The chia seeds act as a thickener while adding healthy omega-3 fatty acids and fiber. You can use this jam on everything—gluten-free toast, waffles, oatmeal, yogurt...honestly, everything. Sweeten it with whatever sugar or alternative sweetener you like. We call for stevia, but maple syrup would be delightful too.

USED IN: **Anytime Almond Biscuits (page 274)**

1½ cups frozen wild blueberries

2 tablespoons water

3 tablespoons chia seeds

¼ teaspoon pure powdered stevia

Squeeze of lemon juice

Warm the blueberries and water in a small saucepan over low heat until the berries are fully defrosted. Remove the pan from the heat.

Using an immersion blender or a muddler, pulse or crush the fruit to your desired consistency.

Add the remaining ingredients and stir to combine. Transfer to a 12-ounce mason jar and let stand uncovered until cool, about 30 minutes. The jam should thicken considerably as the chia seeds hydrate.

Cover and place in the refrigerator to set for at least 4 hours or overnight before using. The jam will keep for up to 10 days in the refrigerator.

CASHEW CHEESE SPREAD

Cashews are extremely versatile in a healthy kitchen. They are rich in fiber and healthy fat and are a great source of plant protein. Use this dairy-free cheese substitute as a base for a dip, a topping for a soup, or a delicious spread for pizza.

USED IN: **Tomato Confit Toast (page 66), Pizza & Sauce (page 70), Portobello Tartlettes (page 212)**

2 cups raw cashews

Filtered water, for soaking cashews

½ to ¾ cup water, to achieve desired consistency

½ cup nutritional yeast

3 tablespoons fresh lemon juice

1 teaspoon salt

1 teaspoon garlic powder

Submerge the cashews in filtered water and place in the refrigerator to soak overnight or for at least 6 hours.

Drain and rinse the cashews.

Put the cashews and ½ cup of water in a food processor. Add the rest of the ingredients and pulse until you have achieved a smooth, ricotta cheese–like texture. If the mixture is too thick, add up to ¼ cup more water.

Store in the refrigerator for up to 10 days.

SPROUTED WALNUTS

This recipe has become a Blais family staple. Don't be afraid of the name; like other sprouted foods, sprouted nuts are easier to digest than raw ones, and your gut absorbs their nutrients faster. The name is a bit of a misnomer because unlike grains and legumes, walnuts don't actually sprout; the process here consists of two simple steps: soaking and dehydrating. For the drying step, you can use a regular oven or a dehydrator, if you have one (see the Note below). Either way, they don't take a lot of work! In the end, we like the texture of these better than raw walnuts. My secret refrigerator snack (you know...the kind you eat standing in front of the open fridge door while no one is watching) is two whole sprouted walnuts, a little butter, and a couple of Thompson raisins. Pile it up like a sandwich and you have a decent stand-in for an oatmeal cookie (in my opinion)—try it yourself to experience the magic of this combination. These tasty and satisfying nuts make a great addition to any trail mix, salad, or quick bread.

USED IN: **Thanksgiving-Style Baked Sweet Potatoes (page 110), A Nice Spinach Salad (page 122), Gluten-Free Carrot Cake (page 196), Buckwheat Pancakes (page 250), Chickpea "Tuna" Salad (page 256)**

2 cups raw walnuts

Filtered water, for soaking

1 tablespoon salt

Rinse the walnuts in a colander under cool running water for about 2 minutes to remove sediment and loose debris.

Place the walnuts in a large mixing bowl. Cover the nuts with 4 cups of filtered water or more so they are fully submerged, then stir in the salt. Place in the refrigerator for at least 12 hours or up to 24 hours.

Drain the walnuts and rinse them in a colander under cool running water, working in batches if necessary. Set aside.

Line a sheet pan with parchment paper and top with an oven-safe crosswire-grid wire rack. Spread the walnuts in a single layer on the rack. If you don't have an oven-safe rack, you can lay the nuts directly on the parchment and add dehydration time.

Position an oven rack in the middle of the oven. Turn the oven on to the lowest setting, which is around 165°F for most conventional home ovens. As low as 150°F is appropriate. The lower the temperature, the better it is for the dehydrating process.

NOTE

If you have a dehydrator, you can use it for this process on the Nuts/Seeds setting. The dehydration time for soaked walnuts will be 18 hours or so.

Place the pan in the oven and bake the nuts for 6 hours, then start checking them hourly. You are looking for a snappy texture but no color and no toasty flavor. This will take up to 12 hours, depending on the heat of your oven. Remove from the oven and allow to cool completely. Once cool, store in an airtight container in the refrigerator for up to a week.

CHARRED VEGETABLE SALSA

This is a total pandemic recipe. It was a moment in life when we'd fire up the grill and throw on anything that was in the fridge or garden and char the daylights out of it. Sounds dark, but it was a weird time. Truly, we just enjoyed making this bright veggie salsa that goes well with a steak, a piece of fish, atop a mound of rice, or smeared on a burger bun. If you have a half a zucchini or a quarter of an eggplant, throw that on the grill too. It will only make your salsa better. So many options!

1 medium red bell pepper

1 jalapeño pepper, seeded

1 medium white or red onion, cut into thick rings

2 baseball-sized tomatoes

2 medjool dates, pitted and roughly chopped

2 teaspoons fig vinegar or red wine vinegar

1 tablespoon olive oil, plus more if needed

1½ teaspoons salt

¼ cup roughly chopped fresh cilantro

Preheat a grill or grill pan to high heat. Brush the hot grill grates or pan with olive oil, then add the bell pepper, jalapeño, onion, and tomatoes and char on all sides until blackened and soft. The onion may take a little longer to cook through than the rest.

Transfer the charred vegetables to a blender. Add the dates, vinegar, olive oil, and salt and blend until the mixture has a chunky texture. Add more oil if the mixture isn't turning in the blender.

Add the cilantro and pulse for a few seconds so the cilantro gets finely chopped but not puréed and the whole thing resembles a chunky salsa.

Serve immediately or store in an airtight container in the refrigerator for up to 3 days.

VEGETARIAN DEMI-GLACE

"Bury me in demi-glace" is a thought I've had once or twice in my life. This rich, delicious mother sauce is good on any roasted proteins or vegetables. To make it vegetarian, we have to stray a bit from the traditional procedure and lose the veal stock, but the texture and flavor here are just as compelling.

USED IN: Porcini Omu-lette (page 204)

2 tablespoons ghee

6 ounces portobello or cremini mushrooms, cleaned and destemmed

1 large carrot, scrubbed and diced

1 medium white onion, chopped

1 stalk celery, chopped

1 small Japanese eggplant, diced

3 cloves garlic, peeled and smashed with the side of a knife

2 tablespoons tomato paste

1 tablespoon coconut aminos

4 cups vegetable stock, divided

2 cups dry red wine

1 bouquet garni (2 fresh thyme sprigs, 2 fresh parsley sprigs, and 1 fresh bay leaf)

Heat the ghee in a large pot over medium heat. Add the vegetables and garlic and cook until they get a little color and then soften, 15 to 20 minutes.

Add the tomato paste and coconut aminos and stir to disperse well. Don't worry about beating up the vegetables a bit; this will release more flavor in the final sauce. Cook for an additional 1 to 2 minutes, until you can smell the tomato cooking.

Add 3 cups of the vegetable stock and stir well. Stir in the wine and bouquet garni and simmer uncovered for 30 minutes, or until the sauce has reduced by half.

Strain out the vegetables (save them for snacking or chop them up and serve them as a bruschetta topping) and add the remaining 1 cup of stock to the pot. Continue simmering over medium heat for 45 minutes to 1 hour, until the sauce has thickened dramatically. When it's done, the sauce should coat the back of a serving spoon momentarily. Discard the bouquet garni.

Remove from the heat and set aside until ready to use. Or let stand to cool before refrigerating. The sauce will keep for up to a week; it can also be frozen in small amounts for future use.

BALSAMIC GLAZE

Store-bought versions of this pantry staple have all kinds of unnecessary ingredients, like sugar, gums, and colorings. Here's a simple version that keeps the delicious flavor and consistency of a balsamic glaze without all of the additives.

USED IN: **Caponata Bruschetta (page 228)**

2 cups balsamic vinegar

2 tablespoons honey or other liquid sweetener of choice (optional)

NOTE

To make this glaze vegan, swap the honey for a vegan liquid sweetener, like date syrup.

Bring the vinegar to a boil in a small saucepan over medium-high heat.

Add the sweetener, if using, and stir until it dissolves.

Lower the heat to medium-low and simmer gently for 12 to 15 minutes, until the volume has reduced by half. Once it coats the back of a spoon, remove the pan from the heat and allow the glaze to cool slightly before transferring it to a squeeze bottle or a jar with a well-fitting lid.

The glaze can be stored in the refrigerator for up to a month.

TOMATO

Tom Brady doesn't eat tomatoes, but we do. The main ingredient in one of the most popular condiments and the backbone of some of the world's greatest cuisines (hello, Italy and Mexico), tomatoes are loved around the world. Plus, every novice gardener you know gives them a run. Thirty million of your friends and neighbors harvested them last summer! We love tomatoes. I love tomatoes for all of the reasons above, with the exception of the Tom Brady bit...I was born a Jets fan and remain a Jets fan, tomato disagreements aside.

I'm happy to report that we can settle the argument of whether a tomato is a fruit or a vegetable here; it's a berry, which is technically a fruit, and that's why tomatoes are so abundant in the summer with the rest of your favorite berries. And like some berries, tomatoes can be eaten raw, cooked, stewed, in a jam, on toast, in a tart, and the list goes on and on. There are about 10,000 varieties of tomatoes, but you'll probably find a small fraction of that at your local grocer, and maybe a few more at your local farmers' market. A few of the common varietals and their best uses are listed in the handy chart on the next page.

In the early days, many Westerners stayed away from tomatoes because they were found to be a member of the nightshade family and thought to be poisonous. (This is the reason Tom Brady eschews tomatoes—their status as a nightshade, which is believed to cause inflammation.) Thankfully, a few brave souls tempted fate, and hundreds of years later we have ketchup and pizza. Tomatoes aren't just a fast-food staple; they wield a nutritious punch in any meal. They're a great source of vitamin C, vitamin K, potassium, and manganese. They also contain lycopene, which is an antioxidant and can reduce inflammation.

You should have a few staple tomato recipes in your repertoire because to me tomatoes are synonymous with easy-to-make dishes. Tomatoes are also jam-packed with umami. If you've watched a good amount of food television over the last decade, I guarantee you've heard that word. Over 100 years ago, a Japanese scientist discovered that the amino acid glutamate was the key compound in umami and what gives that quintessential umami flavor to certain foods. In 2002, umami receptors were discovered on the human tongue. Known as the essence of deliciousness, umami is found in mushrooms, aged cheeses, cured meats, shellfish, and tomatoes, to name a few foods. Simply stated, it's what makes many of our favorite meals delicious.

Rotten tomatoes? Not here! The tomato might not be the media darling or the box office star, but it's a hardworking, fast-stepping member of any ensemble. The role it plays in food is understated yet vital to flavor and appeal. Tomatoes play many roles for me, and, to keep the analogy going, you'll find them playing everything from a small speaking part to a lead performance in the following recipes. All are sure to get a round of applause during the curtain call at your table.

TOMATO	DESCRIPTION
Beefsteak	The classic tomato. Big as a baseball and just as American. This is the guy to put on your hamburger or chop up for a quick salsa.
Grape & Cherry	I think of these as salad tomatoes, but they are also great when quickly roasted or tossed in a pasta dish. They are sweet and juicy with a nice pop of texture.
Heirloom	In the summer, I could eat these out of hand like apples. Reds, greens, purples, yellows, stripes—their variations are endless. I barely mess with these guys, using them on a sandwich or salad or eating them sliced with some flaky sea salt.
Roma	These denser-skinned tomatoes are a great choice for sauces. They stand up to a longer cook time, so they also work well in soups and stews.

TOMATO & WATERMELON POKE

For my restaurants, I love designing dishes that feature an ingredient that resembles another ingredient. The French call this feat trompe l'oeil, or "to fool the eye." It starts with a simple observation that leads to a fun approach or a reimagining of a classic idea, like a tuna poke bowl. Here, the inspiration is obvious. Ahi tuna, in all of its beauty, is a bright, almost translucent red, like ripe watermelon. Or indeed, vice versa. I could go deeper into the comparison, as a large watermelon cut across also resembles a large tuna loin cut the same way, with the nature of their identical spiraling striations connecting these ingredients even more. I've never been a fan of fruity savory dishes, so the addition of tomato here helps firmly plant the identity of this dish as a savory one. I'm sure you will identify it as delicious, and that's the real point.

½ cup black garlic shoyu (see Notes)

½ cup ponzu sauce (see Notes)

Juice of 1 lime

2½ cups large diced watermelon

2 large tomatoes, diced

1 avocado, peeled and diced

1½ cups prepared seaweed salad

½ cup toasted pine nuts, plus more for garnish if desired

2 tablespoons toasted sesame seeds, plus more for garnish if desired

1 tablespoon sliced scallions, plus more for garnish if desired

1 tablespoon toasted sesame oil

½ teaspoon salt

In a large mixing bowl, whisk together the shoyu, ponzu, and lime juice. Add the watermelon and tomato to the bowl and toss to coat evenly with the shoyu dressing.

Gently fold in the remaining ingredients, being mindful not to crush the avocado.

Chill the mixture in the refrigerator for an hour or even overnight.

Garnish with additional pine nuts, sesame seeds, and/or scallions, if desired.

NOTES

Shoyu is the term broadly given to Japanese-style soy sauces made from fermented soybeans, wheat, salt, and water. Black garlic shoyu is a specialty ingredient that features the aged, fermented funkiness of black garlic. Black garlic also milds out the bite of fresh garlic with a bit of sweetness. If you can't find it at your local store, then regular shoyu, soy sauce, tamari, or coconut aminos will substitute appropriately.

Ponzu is a classic sauce originating from Japan. It is typically made from rice wine, rice vinegar, bonito (dried tuna) flakes, and citrus juice. It adds a light citrusy flavor and can be found in most grocery stores or online.

The watermelon, tomato, and avocado will all dice easier when cold. So, if you're a plan-ahead person, stick them in the fridge a few hours before you plan to make this dish.

GAZPACHO

It would be hard to find an easier summer meal to throw together in a shorter time than this sharp and vegetal chilled soup. It's a perfect lunch...so perfect I recently spent a full week enjoying it for lunch every day. Here's my base recipe, but you can use it as a road map to personal variation by punching it up with more herbs or spices. It doesn't always have to be soup, either. Blend it smooth and add a splash more vinegar to make a nice vinaigrette, or reduce the oil to 1 tablespoon and leave some chunky texture to make a slamming sauce to toss with grilled vegetables—the opportunities are endless!

2 large ripe slicing tomatoes (beefsteak or other heirloom variety)

1 medium cucumber

½ medium Anaheim chili pepper (see Notes)

2 tablespoons fresh basil or cilantro leaves

1 clove garlic, peeled

3 tablespoons extra-virgin olive oil

3 tablespoons red wine vinegar

1 scant tablespoon salt

½ teaspoon freshly ground black pepper

Roughly chop the tomatoes, cucumber, chili pepper, basil, and garlic and place in a blender. Add the olive oil, vinegar, salt, and black pepper and blend until mostly smooth, about 45 seconds.

Chill the soup in the refrigerator for at least an hour before serving.

NOTES

For the Anaheim chili, you could substitute a jalapeño for more heat or a green bell pepper if it's easier to find.

If you'd like to garnish the soup, try using some of the same vegetables from the soup, finely diced, along with a drizzle of extra-virgin olive oil, a dollop of plain yogurt, and/or more of the fresh herbs.

SHAKSHOUKA
WITH CHICKPEAS & PEPPERS

OPTION

Shakshouka is one of those egg dishes that can be eaten for any meal of the day. Although I think of it as a savory breakfast, its merits can be enjoyed as a quick dinner or late-night excursion. The best part is that you probably have most of these ingredients in the fridge. It could easily be described as an egg dish, but it feels right to feature this recipe in the tomato chapter because the tomato pulls all of the ingredients together into a luscious, saucy dish. You'll want some grilled corn tortillas or toast points on hand to sop up the extra sauce. A few drops of hot sauce would really set breakfast off on the right note.

3 tablespoons olive oil

1 large yellow onion, halved and thinly sliced

1 large red bell pepper, seeded and thinly sliced

3 cloves garlic, thinly sliced

1 teaspoon ground cumin

1 teaspoon paprika

1 (28-ounce) can whole plum tomatoes with juices, roughly chopped

1 (15-ounce) can chickpeas, drained and rinsed

¾ teaspoon salt

¼ teaspoon freshly ground black pepper

6 large eggs

FOR GARNISH

1¼ cups crumbled feta cheese (optional)

½ cup pitted olives of choice

½ cup chopped fresh cilantro

Preheat the oven to 350°F.

In an oven-safe sauté pan or large skillet (cast iron works great here), heat the olive oil over medium-high heat. Once the oil is glassy, add the onion, bell pepper, and garlic and sauté for 3 to 5 minutes, until the onion is translucent.

Reduce the heat to medium, season with the cumin and paprika, and sauté for an additional minute or two, until fragrant.

Add the canned tomatoes with their juices. Stir and bring the mixture to a simmer. Cook, stirring occasionally, until the sauce has thickened slightly.

Fold in the chickpeas and remove the pan from the heat.

Season with the salt and pepper, then taste and adjust the seasoning if needed, keeping in mind the saltiness the feta and olives will bring to the dish.

Using the back of a large spoon, make six divots on the surface of the tomato sauce for the eggs. Gently crack an egg into each divot and bake until the eggs are cooked to your desired doneness—15 to 20 minutes will yield medium-done eggs with solid whites and runny yolks.

Remove the pan from the oven and top the shakshouka with the feta, if desired, and the olives and cilantro.

NOTE
To make this recipe dairy free, omit the feta or use a plant-based alternative.

TOMATO CONFIT TOAST

WITH CASHEW CHEESE

Here's a version of pan con tomate, a staple in the Spanish lexicon. Traditionally, it can be as simple as a toasted piece of bread with a spread of tomato pulp. In this recipe, we're cooking some cherry tomatoes confit. *Confit* simply means "with fat" in French, but because tomatoes have very little fat of their own, we'll add some good olive oil and let them bake in those juices until tender. I serve these toasts with a schmear of cashew cheese, which is a more than capable stand-in for ricotta (one of my favorite dairy spreads) if you're going dairy free.

2 pints cherry tomatoes, washed and dried

Salt and pepper

3 tablespoons olive oil

2 sprigs fresh thyme

½ cup Cashew Cheese Spread (page 46)

4 slices sourdough or gluten-free bread, toasted

Torn fresh basil, flat-leaf parsley, or mint leaves, for garnish (optional)

Preheat the oven to 325°F. Line a sheet pan with aluminum foil.

Put the tomatoes on the prepared sheet pan and sprinkle them liberally with salt and pepper. Add the olive oil and thyme sprigs and shake to coat evenly.

Roast for 1 hour, or until the tomatoes have shriveled and deflated substantially. Set aside.

Spread the cashew cheese on the toasted bread and top with a spoonful of the tomato confit.

Drizzle some of the remaining olive oil from the sheet pan over the toast. If desired, garnish with some torn basil, parsley, or mint leaves.

NOTES
To make this recipe gluten free, use gluten-free bread for the toast. To ensure that it is vegan, use a bread labeled certified vegan.

THE TOMATO
WITH YUZU & SHISO

There are times as a professional chef when I need to take a step back and refresh my perspective. A few times a year, I challenge myself to remove certain items from my daily diet. The shift that occurs when I am pushed outside of my comfort zone is always a source of inspiration and creativity in the kitchen. Once I removed sugar for six weeks, and as a cook it reset my palate so I could appreciate the natural sweetness of a carrot or tomato. Growing some of your own food can also change your perspective. A tomato is beautiful in its simplicity; it doesn't need much. This dish is the love child of both of those experiences, highlighting and illustrating where I'm trying very hard not to try too hard. This is a salad, a ceviche or crudo, if you want to call it that. It's a perfect side for a grilled steak, or just a tomato. *THE* tomato!

4 beefsteak tomatoes

¼ cup yuzu juice (see Notes)

2 tablespoons extra-virgin olive oil

1½ teaspoons toasted sesame oil

1 tablespoon white soy sauce (see Notes)

2 tablespoons sliced scallions, plus more for garnish if desired

½ teaspoon peeled and grated fresh ginger

Salt and pepper

12 fresh shiso leaves, or 24 fresh basil leaves, plus more for garnish if desired

2 tablespoons black sesame seeds, for garnish (optional)

Cut each tomato crosswise in ¼-inch slices. (Think thick sandwich slices.) Keep the slices together for each tomato.

Make a simple vinaigrette by whisking together the yuzu juice, olive oil, sesame oil, soy sauce, scallions, and ginger until emulsified.

Season each tomato slice with a little salt and pepper and spoon some vinaigrette over each slice.

Reassemble each tomato to look whole, sandwiching the shiso leaves between the slices. Drizzle with any remaining vinaigrette and garnish with scallions, shiso leaves, and/or black sesame seeds, if desired.

NOTES

Yuzu juice, from a Japanese citrus fruit with notes of lemon and pine, was once hard to source. Now it can be found pretty readily at fancier grocery stores. If you have a hard time tracking it down, try a mixture of lemon and orange juice stirred with a sprig of rosemary.

Being a clear liquid, white soy sauce is a fun ingredient to use in a composed salad like this one since the fermented punch comes as surprise. If you can't find it, regular soy sauce or coconut aminos is a fine replacement.

PIZZA & SAUCE

Here's the biggest confession in this book (so far): I've failed terribly so, so, so many times at making pizza. Trying to use fancy doughs, making said dough too thin, breaking the dough, undercooking the center of the pie—the complete list of my failures is especially long. However, this is the easiest and most unorthodox dough recipe you'll find. One that doesn't require rising, proofing, or stretching. One that even I make regularly with success! Now, to be clear, this recipe will have pizza purists (you know who you are) raising their eyebrows. Pizzaiolos and my Italian friends will not even identify this as pizza dough, and that's before I put pineapple on it! But it works, and conveniently it has a few more health benefits than traditional dough.

FOR THE SAUCE

(Makes 1 quart)

4 cups canned crushed tomatoes

¼ cup finely diced white onions

1 teaspoon dried oregano leaves

1 fresh basil leaf

FOR THE DOUGH

1 cup self-rising flour, plus more for dusting the work surface

1 cup cottage cheese

Pinch of salt

TOPPINGS

1 cup shredded mozzarella cheese or vegan mozzarella shreds

10 to 12 fresh basil leaves, chopped

Red pepper flakes (optional)

TO MAKE THE SAUCE:

Combine the tomatoes, onions, and oregano in a medium-sized saucepan and simmer for about 25 minutes to allow the flavors to develop and the sauce to thicken.

Remove the pan from the heat and add the basil leaf. Once cool, transfer the sauce to an airtight glass container and store in the refrigerator until needed. It will keep for up to 10 days. Alternatively, after it has cooled, it can be frozen for up to 2 months.

TO MAKE THE CRUSTS AND PIZZAS:

Preheat the oven to 450°F. Grease a baking sheet.

Put the flour, cottage cheese, and salt in a food processor and pulse until a dough ball forms. You may need to scrape down the sides of the bowl intermittently.

Turn the dough out onto a lightly dusted work surface and divide the dough in half. Using your hands, roll each half loosely into a ball. If the dough is too sticky, flour your hands as well. Reflour the surface and your hands as necessary.

Using a floured rolling pin, roll each ball into a ¼-inch-thick round. Transfer the dough rounds to the prepared baking sheet.

Top each pizza with 3 tablespoons or more of the sauce, half of the cheese, and half of the chopped basil.

Bake the pizzas for 15 to 20 minutes, until the crust is golden
brown and the cheese is melted. Serve immediately, topped with
red pepper flakes if desired.

SPAGHETTI POMODORO
WITH OLIVES, CAPERS & ANCHOVIES

OPTION

We wanted to include a tomato-based pasta sauce in this book and thought awhile about which one to feature. Pasta is my go-to answer to the oft-asked interview question of what I would eat if I had to choose one food for the rest of my life. It's also an easy fix for busy working parents. At first I worried that pomodoro in its authentic state was too simple... but no, simple is delicious. Simple can be difficult too because there's nowhere to hide. So here's a simple dish! If you want to use zucchini noodles (you can buy them in select groceries now, or use a mandoline to create thin linguine-like shapes), this becomes a powerhouse of a healthy meal. We use gluten-free spaghetti, which has come along light-years since its inception. Try a few brands and find your favorite!

1 pound gluten-free or whole-wheat spaghetti

2 tablespoons olive oil

2 cups halved fresh cherry tomatoes, or 1 (12-ounce) can cherry tomatoes

½ teaspoon red pepper flakes, or ⅛ teaspoon Calabrian chili oil

½ teaspoon anchovy paste

3 tablespoons sliced green olives

1 tablespoon capers, drained

½ cup chopped fresh basil, divided

Salt and pepper

Cook the spaghetti per the package instructions for al dente. Drain and set aside. Do not rinse the pasta.

In a sauté pan, warm the olive oil over medium heat. Add the tomatoes (if using canned, drain off most of the juices) and red pepper flakes and cook for 2 minutes, until the tomatoes shrivel and start melting into the oil.

Stir in the anchovy paste until it is fully incorporated and no large chunks remain.

Remove the pan from the heat and stir in the olives, capers, and ¼ cup of the basil. Season to taste with salt and pepper.

Add the pasta to the pan and use tongs or a fork to fold it into the sauce until coated.

Serve in bowls, garnished with the remaining basil.

NOTE
To make this recipe gluten free, use a gluten-free spaghetti.

"CINCINNATI-STYLE" MEATLESS CHILI

   OPTION OPTION

I put this recipe in the book for two reasons. One, to validate my legacy as a road warrior and flavor explorer. Cincinnati is one of my favorite cities for a long run. If you chart it properly, you can trot across a few majestic bridges and brag that you ran through two states. Two, I love Cincinnati chili and its remarkable spice blend. Double this recipe and freeze it, and relish in the uniqueness that is Cincinnati chili and its toppings. Also, we're using "alternative plant-based beef" here because this is the type of application where it can shine as the vehicle for a sauce rather than as the main character. We serve it over spaghetti and top it with raw onions for that traditional Cincinnati chili experience. You could also serve it over rice. It makes a great hot dog topping too, even for vegan dogs or Charred Carrot Hot Dogs (page 190).

FOR THE SEASONING MIX

¼ cup chili powder

1 tablespoon coconut sugar

1 tablespoon salt

1 teaspoon garlic powder

1 teaspoon ground cinnamon

¼ teaspoon allspice

¼ teaspoon ground cloves

¼ teaspoon red pepper flakes (see Notes)

⅛ teaspoon freshly ground black pepper

2 tablespoons ghee or olive oil

1¼ pounds Impossible Beef, Beyond Beef, or your favorite plant-based ground meat

1 (6-ounce) can tomato paste

5 cups water

2 tablespoons apple cider vinegar

½ ounce unsweetened baking chocolate, roughly chopped

FOR SERVING

1 pound gluten-free or whole-wheat spaghetti, cooked per package instructions

½ cup chopped white onions

Stir together all of the seasoning mix ingredients.

In a large heavy-bottomed saucepot with tall sides, heat the ghee over medium-high heat until smoking. Add the "meat" and sear for a few minutes, breaking up the larger pieces with a wooden spoon.

Add the seasoning mix and tomato paste, stir to incorporate, and continue to cook for another few minutes.

Add the water, vinegar, and chocolate and simmer, uncovered, until the volume has reduced by one-quarter and the flavors have developed, 30 minutes to 1 hour.

Serve over the spaghetti and top with the onions.

NOTES

This is a chili with some depth and a touch of heat. The red pepper flakes are used to counterbalance the sweetness of the other ingredients. If you are sensitive to spicy food, reduce the red pepper flakes to ⅛ teaspoon.

To make this recipe gluten free, serve the chili over gluten-free spaghetti or rice. To make it vegan, use olive oil rather than ghee for the pan.

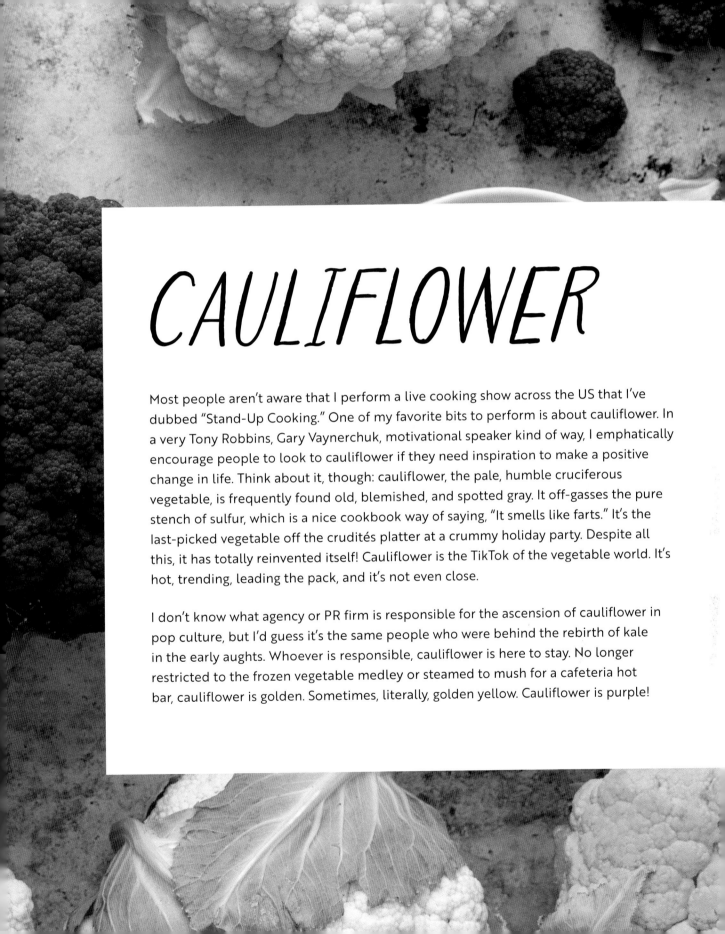

CAULIFLOWER

Most people aren't aware that I perform a live cooking show across the US that I've dubbed "Stand-Up Cooking." One of my favorite bits to perform is about cauliflower. In a very Tony Robbins, Gary Vaynerchuk, motivational speaker kind of way, I emphatically encourage people to look to cauliflower if they need inspiration to make a positive change in life. Think about it, though: cauliflower, the pale, humble cruciferous vegetable, is frequently found old, blemished, and spotted gray. It off-gasses the pure stench of sulfur, which is a nice cookbook way of saying, "It smells like farts." It's the last-picked vegetable off the crudités platter at a crummy holiday party. Despite all this, it has totally reinvented itself! Cauliflower is the TikTok of the vegetable world. It's hot, trending, leading the pack, and it's not even close.

I don't know what agency or PR firm is responsible for the ascension of cauliflower in pop culture, but I'd guess it's the same people who were behind the rebirth of kale in the early aughts. Whoever is responsible, cauliflower is here to stay. No longer restricted to the frozen vegetable medley or steamed to mush for a cafeteria hot bar, cauliflower is golden. Sometimes, literally, golden yellow. Cauliflower is purple!

Cauliflower is mashed potatoes! Cauliflower is rice! Cauliflower is pizza dough! Heresy! Cauliflower is even served as steak! Cauliflower is endorsed by Oprah! Cauliflower is having a moment! So, naturally, how could we ignore this superstar, especially in a book based on healthy plant-forward eating?

Cauliflower is not all fluff and publicity. It's got the verified credentials of a true superfood. In fact, the very same molecule that gives it that gassy smell also gives it a big antioxidant kick. So, besides fighting inflammation, cauliflower helps brain health, gut health, and hormone regulation. The kid can do it all!

It's an incredibly versatile ingredient. A blank canvas. One that absorbs flavor and can transmute into any cuisine, especially flavor-forward ones like Indian, Asian, and North African. Cauliflower is a rare vegetable that purées easily without becoming textureless or watery. It mimics the simplicity of potato or parsnip in a smooth mash. It can be vegetable, starch, or even protein. When our now-teenager was a baby, I worked with a frozen baby food company and created a flavor with a cauliflower base. It was called Goin' Back to Cauli, and it worked because of its texture but also its approachability. There's a training wheel approach when it comes to cauliflower. I think you could make even the most ardent anti-vegetable character eat something with cauliflower in it— the fail-safe is a smoothie, but there are so many options.

So here's a chapter devoted to cauliflower, the do-it-all vegetable. And, yes, we all know what's next: cauliflower, THE PODCAST!!!

CREAMY CAULIFLOWER & COCONUT SOUP

SERVES 4

OPTION   OPTION OPTION

Here's a healthier take on the classic cream of cauliflower soup. It's a simple and elegant dish—just right for when the air turns a little crisp and you want that comforting hug you get from "cream of" soups. I'm not adding any exotic spices here; it's perfect in its simplicity. That being said, some Jamaican curry powder is a lovely addition if you want to move away from the traditional.

Florets from 1 large head cauliflower, chopped into small chunks

2 cups chicken or vegetable stock

2 cups plain unsweetened coconut milk (see Notes)

Salt and ground white pepper

1 tablespoon coconut aminos

3 tablespoons unsalted butter or ghee (optional; see Notes)

¼ cup gluten-free croutons, toasted, for garnish

¼ cup finely diced apples, for garnish

Put the cauliflower, stock, and coconut milk in a small stockpot over medium-high heat. Cook until the cauliflower is tender, about 20 minutes.

Season with salt and pepper to taste.

Working in batches if needed, pour the mixture into a blender and blend until silky smooth.

Return the soup to the pot and stir in the coconut aminos. Adjust the seasoning to taste with salt and pepper.

Swirl in the butter, if using, and melt over low heat, stirring to combine.

Ladle into serving bowls and garnish with the toasted croutons and diced apples.

NOTES

The type of coconut milk you want here is the refrigerated type sold in cartons, not the canned shelf-stable type.

Butter or ghee adds another layer of creaminess to this soup that I enjoy. You could reduce the amount by half or omit it altogether and have a perfectly passable dairy-free bowl.

To make this recipe vegetarian, use vegetable stock; to make it vegan, also omit the butter or ghee.

CAULIFLOWER FRIED RICE

OPTION

Sure, there are packaged versions of this very dish, but you can make your own with pretty minimal effort and dodge a whole bunch of sodium and additives. I love that. We are definitely using frozen riced cauliflower here because it's easy to find and not much different than if you were to rice your own cauliflower. The rest comes through like the fried rice you made in college (or I did, at least)—delicious, simple, and healthier than the original. Leftovers? They can be used in the Porcini Omu-lette recipe (page 204).

2 tablespoons toasted sesame oil, divided

2 large eggs, beaten with a pinch of salt

1 tablespoon olive oil

1 tablespoon white miso

½ medium yellow onion, finely diced

3 cloves garlic, minced

1 tablespoon peeled and grated fresh ginger

1 (8-ounce) package sliced white button mushrooms

½ cup grated carrots or carrots cut into matchsticks

2 (12-ounce) bags frozen riced cauliflower, thawed

1 cup frozen green peas, thawed

2 tablespoons soy sauce or coconut aminos

1 teaspoon rice vinegar

Sesame seeds, for topping

Sliced scallions, for topping

In a wok or a large cast-iron skillet, heat 1 tablespoon of the sesame oil over medium heat. Add the eggs, stir, and cook for about 2 minutes, until the eggs are just set. Remove to a bowl and set aside.

Return the pan to the heat and add the remaining tablespoon of sesame oil, the olive oil, and the miso. Add the onion, garlic, and ginger and sauté, stirring often, until softened, 3 to 4 minutes. Add the mushrooms and carrots and continue to cook until the vegetables are softened and lightly browned, 5 to 7 minutes.

Add the "rice" and peas and toss thoroughly with the rest of the vegetables and sauce. Stir in the soy sauce and vinegar. Return the eggs to the pan and use a wooden spoon to break up the pieces and disperse them. Continue to cook until everything is hot and cooked through.

Serve in bowls, topped with sesame seeds and sliced scallions.

NOTE
To make this recipe gluten free, use coconut aminos rather than soy sauce.

CAULIFLOWER NUGGETS

WITH BUFFALO SAUCE & QUICK PICKLED VEGETABLES

Buffalo cauliflower took the internet by storm a few years back. Unlike a lot of recent internet trends, this one has some serious credibility and staying power. It's giving finger-licking tailgate dish vibes...but made healthy! Here we are baking, not frying, plus increasing the nutritious plant content by substituting cauliflower for chicken, so it's a much healthier snack all around. When served as a snack, it will feed four, but you are welcome to make this a meal for two instead! Serve with Richie's Ranch Dressing (page 28).

FOR THE NUGGETS

1 large head cauliflower, broken into golf ball–size florets

2 tablespoons olive oil

1½ teaspoons salt

½ teaspoon freshly ground black pepper

FOR THE PICKLES

¼ cup sliced carrots

¼ cup sliced celery

½ jalapeño pepper, sliced

½ cup distilled white vinegar, plus more if needed

FOR THE BUFFALO SAUCE

½ cup Frank's RedHot Original sauce

2 tablespoons unsalted butter, melted

¼ cup crumbled blue cheese, for garnish (optional)

Preheat the oven to 400°F. Have on hand a nonstick sheet pan, or line a regular one with parchment paper.

Toss the cauliflower in the olive oil and season with the salt and pepper. Spread the cauliflower on the pan and roast until just tender, 30 to 40 minutes.

While the cauliflower is cooking, make the pickles: Combine the carrots, celery, and jalapeño with ½ cup of the vinegar in a glass or nonreactive metal container, making sure the vegetables are completely submerged. Add more vinegar if needed.

Make the Buffalo sauce: In a large mixing bowl, whisk together the hot sauce and melted butter.

Remove the cauliflower from the oven once tender and add it to the bowl with the Buffalo sauce. Toss to coat evenly.

Drain the pickled vegetables. Garnish the cauliflower nuggets with the pickled vegetables and the blue cheese, if desired.

CAULIFLOWER WHITE PIZZA

WITH CASHEW CHEESE, TRUFFLE OIL & MUSHROOMS

My history with making pizza is tragic, but this recipe is foolproof. Plus, it's cauliflower on cauliflower, doubling the nutritional content of this powerhouse vegetable! Our teenager actually prefers cauliflower pizza to the traditional kind when it's made at home...but that may be due more to my many bungled efforts with traditional dough. We suggest making the cashew cheese ahead of time, as it can keep for over a week. Then, when you're ready for a pizza night, you just need to assemble the crust and toppings and turn on the oven. Alternatively, this dough can topped like a flatbread with a copious drizzle of olive oil and some chopped fresh parsley or basil.

FOR THE PIZZA DOUGH

2 tablespoons flax seeds, ground

¼ cup room-temperature water

Salt

1 large head cauliflower

½ cup brown rice flour, plus more for rolling out the dough

1 tablespoon arrowroot powder (optional; see Notes, page 88)

1 teaspoon garlic powder

1 teaspoon onion powder

1 tablespoon Italian seasoning or dried oregano leaves

FOR THE CAULIFLOWER 'BÉCHAMEL'

3 cups cauliflower florets, chopped

2½ cups plain unsweetened almond milk

2 tablespoons nutritional yeast (optional; see Notes)

1 teaspoon salt

½ teaspoon ground white pepper

⅛ teaspoon dried thyme leaves

FOR THE SAUTÉED MUSHROOMS

1 cup white button mushrooms

2 tablespoons ghee or olive oil

2 tablespoons finely chopped fresh parsley, plus more for garnish

1 teaspoon white truffle oil

½ teaspoon fresh lemon juice

Salt and ground white pepper

1 cup Cashew Cheese Spread (page 46)

TO MAKE THE CRUST:

Combine the ground flax seeds and room-temperature water in a small bowl. Stir vigorously for 30 seconds, then set aside for 5 minutes. The mixture will become slightly frothy and thicken upon standing (see Notes).

Bring a large pot of salted water to a boil. Chop the cauliflower into small florets and boil until tender. Drain and pulse in a food processor until granular.

Place the cauliflower in a fine-mesh strainer and press with the back of a large spoon to remove the excess moisture. Alternatively, wring the cauliflower in a clean dish towel or cheesecloth to remove as much liquid as possible. This step is imperative to getting a dough that crisps when cooked.

In a medium-sized mixing bowl, combine the cauliflower pulp, flour, arrowroot, flax seed mixture, spices, and 1 teaspoon of salt to form a dense dough that holds its shape. (This can be done up to 5 days ahead; place the dough in an airtight container or wrap it in plastic wrap and store it in the refrigerator.)

Preheat the oven to 375°F.

Divide the dough into two equal portions and, using your hands, roll each into a ball. Thoroughly dust a clean, smooth work surface and rolling pin with rice flour. Roll out each dough ball to a ⅛-inch-thick round about 6 inches in diameter.

Transfer the rounds to parchment paper and place on a sheet pan.

Par-bake the crusts for 45 minutes. Remove the crusts from the oven and loosen them from the parchment paper with a spatula. Place another piece of parchment on top of the crusts. Very carefully flip the crusts, remove the parchment that is now on top, and bake for another 10 minutes, until the center is mostly firm and the edges are set and golden. Keep the crusts on the pan until ready to add toppings.

(The crusts can be frozen after being par-baked. Allow them to cool completely, then place in an airtight container and freeze for up to a month.)

TO MAKE THE BÉCHAMEL:

Combine the cauliflower, almond milk, nutritional yeast (if using), salt, pepper, and thyme in a large saucepan and simmer uncovered until the cauliflower is tender.

Transfer the hot cauliflower and half of the milk from the pan to a blender or food processor. Blend into a smooth puree and use as you would a traditional béchamel. Add more of the milk as necessary to achieve a thick and luscious saucy texture—think queso!

Store leftover béchamel in an airtight container in the refrigerator for up to 5 days.

TO PREPARE THE MUSHROOMS:

Clean the mushrooms and cut into ¼- to ½-inch slices.

Heat the ghee in a sauté pan over medium heat. Add the mushrooms and sauté for 2 minutes, then add the parsley. Continue to sauté for 4 to 7 minutes more, until the mushrooms are tender.

Remove the pan from the heat and stir in the truffle oil and lemon juice. Season with salt and pepper to taste.

TO ASSEMBLE THE PIZZAS:

Preheat the oven to 500°F.

Using about ½ cup of cashew cheese per pizza, spread a thin layer on each crust, leaving a 1-inch border, and dot each pizza with a few tablespoons of the cauliflower béchamel. Top with the mushrooms, dividing them evenly between the pizzas.

Bake the pizzas for 10 to 15 minutes, until the toppings are bubbly and hot and the crust is lightly browned. Garnish with parsley and serve.

NOTES

The flax egg, as it is known, is comprised of ground flax seeds and water and used as an egg replacement in vegan recipes; we are relying on its binding ability here for the dough.

Arrowroot powder, a cornstarch alternative, helps bind and thicken. If you find the dough to be looser than cottage cheese, you will need to include the arrowroot powder (or cornstarch) or add a bit more flour.

Nutritional yeast is a hack for vegan chefs to add a savory, cheesy, umami flavor without any meat products, salt, sugar, or fat. It has a nutty savoriness similar to Swiss cheese that we enjoy.

To make this recipe vegan, use olive oil rather than ghee for the mushrooms.

JERK-SPICED CAULIFLOWER STEAKS

OPTION

This shouldn't cause alarm, but cauliflower can be steak. If it can be rice, pizza, and pasta, then it can definitely stand in for a main dish. Eggplant would be another fun turn using this idea of making a thick slab of vegetable the star of dinner. Jerk spice is a common blend from the Caribbean consisting mainly of allspice and peppers. It's a spicy-sweet mix that is a distant cousin to the curry powders and garam masalas of the world.

FOR THE JERK SPICE GLAZE
(Makes about ¼ cup)

½ teaspoon allspice berries

¼ teaspoon black peppercorns

½ cup olive oil, plus more if needed

2 tablespoons coconut aminos

2 tablespoons coconut sugar

1 tablespoon apple cider vinegar

Leaves from 3 sprigs fresh thyme

2 bay leaves

2 scallions, chopped

Grated zest and juice of 1 lime

1 Fresno chili pepper, seeded

1 (2-inch) piece fresh ginger, peeled and sliced

1 clove garlic, peeled

1 shallot, chopped

½ teaspoon prepared yellow mustard

½ Scotch bonnet chili pepper, seeded

½ teaspoon freshly grated nutmeg

¼ teaspoon ground cinnamon

FOR THE CAULIFLOWER STEAKS

1 large head cauliflower, cut from top to stem into four 2- to 3-inch-thick slices

1 tablespoon salt

Ghee, olive oil, or grapeseed oil, for the pan

Fresh cilantro or parsley leaves, for garnish (optional)

Preheat the oven to 400°F.

Using a spice grinder, grind the allspice berries and peppercorns to a powder.

To make the glaze, put the ground spices and all of the remaining glaze ingredients in a high-powered blender or food processor and blend until completely smooth. Add more olive oil if needed to process.

Season the cauliflower steaks with the salt.

Heat a large cast-iron or other heavy-bottomed skillet over medium-high heat. Melt 2 tablespoons of ghee in the pan.

Working in batches, sear the "steaks" until golden brown on both sides, about 3 minutes per side, adding another tablespoon of ghee to the pan for each new batch.

Brush the glaze liberally on all sides of the "steaks." Place on a nonstick sheet pan and bake until tender, 15 to 20 minutes. Garnish with fresh herbs.

ROASTED WHOLE HEAD OF CAULIFLOWER

WITH AROMATICS & SULTANAS

I created the flavor profiles of this recipe like I do for a lot of the recipes I develop. Inspired by the term "head of cauliflower," my thoughts immediately went to traditional goat head recipes from India, the Caribbean, or Mexico. Then, in a small leap, I arrived at a dish imbued with the luscious flavors of garam masala, coriander, and similar spices. You can adjust the seasonings here and add sliced jalapeños or chipotle powder to provide some heat, but this is how we serve it at home. This dish is a Blais family staple. We love this riff because it can be served as a meal or a family-style side. Jazmin likes to cook the cauliflower a little past fork-tender so it can be spooned easily at the dinner table.

1 large head cauliflower

¼ cup olive oil or ghee

2 to 3 cloves garlic, minced

1 tablespoon peeled and minced fresh ginger

2 teaspoons garam masala (see Note)

1 teaspoon turmeric powder

A couple grinds of black pepper

1 teaspoon salt

2 tablespoons unsalted butter

½ lemon

¼ cup chopped fresh parsley

2 tablespoons chopped fresh cilantro

2 tablespoons sultanas (aka golden raisins)

Preheat the oven to 375°F.

Remove the leaves from the cauliflower and wash the head. Remove the stem up to the florets to create a flat base for the head to sit on. Place the head of cauliflower in a Dutch oven with a lid.

Warm the olive oil in a small saucepan over medium heat. Add the garlic, ginger, spices, and salt and stir to incorporate thoroughly in the oil. Cook, stirring often, until fragrant, about 3 minutes, then remove the pan from the heat.

Using a pastry brush or your hands (after allowing the oil to cool to the touch), coat the entire cauliflower head with the spiced oil, brushing or massaging it into each crevice from top to bottom.

Place the lid on the Dutch oven and set on the middle rack in the oven. Cook for 40 minutes.

Remove the lid and cook for an additional 30 to 40 minutes, or until the cauliflower is golden brown on the outside and fork-tender.

In a small sauté pan, melt the butter over medium heat until the solids start to separate and the frothiness recedes. The butter should be light brown in color and smell of toasted hazelnuts.

Remove the pan from the heat and squeeze the juice of half a lemon into the butter. Add the parsley, cilantro, and sultanas and swirl to mix. Set aside, keeping warm until the cauliflower is ready to serve.

Transfer the cauliflower to a serving plate and drizzle with the butter mixture.

Garam masala is an easy-to-find spice blend that is widely used in India and southeast Asia. It typically contains cinnamon, coriander, cumin, mace, peppercorns, and other warm spices.

CAULI-MAC 'N' CHEESE

SERVES 4 TO 6

OPTION

Life is about balance. Would I like to eat a giant bowl of ooey-gooey macaroni and cheese every night? Sure! Would my body love that? Probably not. This recipe gives your body a little more to love. As we've discussed at length, cauliflower can do it all; here, it's asked to be a white sauce, adding creaminess, depth, and a bit of texture to the traditional recipe. And I'll be honest, I don't miss the dairy milk here. The savoriness of cashew milk or even barley milk makes it the proper choice for this dish.

1 pound gluten-free or whole-wheat elbow macaroni

Florets from 1 medium head cauliflower, roughly chopped

2 cups chicken or vegetable stock

2 cups plain unsweetened cashew or barley milk

1 teaspoon nutritional yeast

1 shallot, peeled

1 whole clove

1 bay leaf

1 cup shredded white cheddar cheese

1 cup shredded mozzarella cheese

½ cup grated Parmesan cheese

2 teaspoons salt

1 teaspoon ground white pepper

1 cup gluten-free breadcrumbs

2 tablespoons unsalted butter or ghee

½ cup fresh parsley leaves, chopped, for garnish

Preheat the oven to 375°F.

Cook the macaroni per the package instructions for al dente. Drain and set aside. Do not rinse the pasta.

Put the cauliflower, stock, milk, nutritional yeast, shallot, clove, and bay leaf in a large heavy-bottomed saucepan over medium heat. Cook until the cauliflower is fork-tender, about 15 minutes. Remove the pan from the heat and spoon out the clove and bay leaf.

Working in batches if needed, pour the cauliflower, shallot, and cooking liquid into a blender and blend until smooth.

Return the cauliflower puree to the saucepan and bring to a gentle simmer over medium-low heat. Gradually whisk in the cheeses. Season with the salt and pepper. The mixture should thicken up considerably.

Fold in the cooked macaroni and transfer to a 13 by 9-inch baking dish. Top with the breadcrumbs and dot with the butter.

Bake until the top is golden and bubbly, 10 to 15 minutes. Garnish with the chopped parsley and serve immediately.

NOTE
To make this recipe gluten free, use a gluten-free macaroni.

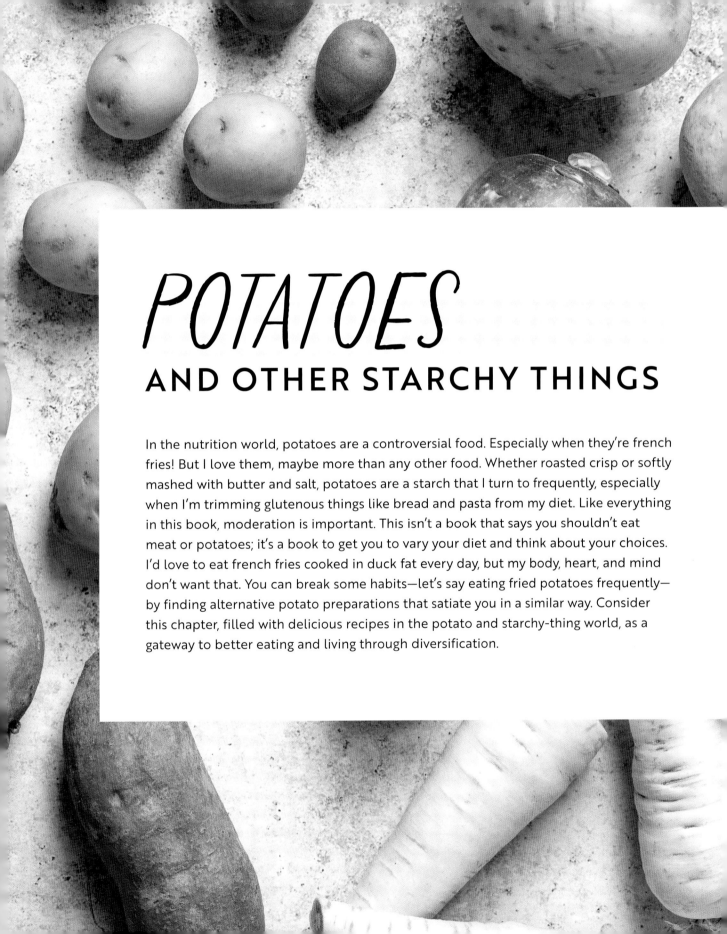

POTATOES
AND OTHER STARCHY THINGS

In the nutrition world, potatoes are a controversial food. Especially when they're french fries! But I love them, maybe more than any other food. Whether roasted crisp or softly mashed with butter and salt, potatoes are a starch that I turn to frequently, especially when I'm trimming glutenous things like bread and pasta from my diet. Like everything in this book, moderation is important. This isn't a book that says you shouldn't eat meat or potatoes; it's a book to get you to vary your diet and think about your choices. I'd love to eat french fries cooked in duck fat every day, but my body, heart, and mind don't want that. You can break some habits—let's say eating fried potatoes frequently— by finding alternative potato preparations that satiate you in a similar way. Consider this chapter, filled with delicious recipes in the potato and starchy-thing world, as a gateway to better eating and living through diversification.

In fact, I bet you'll find recipes here that aren't just substitutions for fries but ones you'll end up preferring and having on the dinner table regularly.

This reminds me of when I quit drinking diet soda, or any soda, really. I was a diet soda head, drinking at least two cans a day. I struggle with willpower like everyone else, but when I set my mind to it and say "no more," it's easy for me to move on. I know I'm lucky in this way. I kicked my soda habit cold turkey. At first, I replaced that daily bubbly sensation with club soda. It satiated my need for a carbonated beverage, although it wasn't as exciting as a fountain drink from the nearest gas station. Then I switched to flavored carbonated beverages with no calories and haven't looked back. I enjoy the lightness of seltzer. The few times I've sipped a soda in the last eight years, I've been surprised at how sticky-sweet it can be.

Because the trouble with potatoes is that they are often fried, we are taking the opportunity in this chapter to open some other avenues for potato consumption. After all, whole civilizations' meal planning has been based on potatoes. Ever heard of the Incas in Peru? Four thousand varieties of potatoes were grown above 3,000 feet in the Andes Mountains. Crazy! There's even a National Potato Day in Peru, celebrated every year on the thirtieth of May. Yes, I just added this event to my bucket list. The point is, the Incas weren't eating french fries. They were mashing, roasting, and fermenting this starchy goodness for hundreds of years. There are lots of ways to enjoy this tuber— plus, it's loaded with vitamin C and is pretty easy to grow. Our daughters grew them in their school garden in second grade. Not a gardener? No problem! Potatoes are widely available and pretty economical.

In this chapter, you'll also find sweet potatoes, parsnip, turnips, and rutabaga. Sweet potatoes are generally regarded as the healthier potato (compared to white potatoes). They are a classic superfood with lots of beneficial vitamins and minerals, plus they're filling and will satiate that carb craving. Some of the other tubers, roots, and starches used in this chapter can be interchanged easily. They all offer good nutritional benefits and are readily found in supermarkets.

Being starchy, most of the recipes in the chapter are meant to be served as side dishes, to be enjoyed in moderation along with a lovely salad or a lean piece of protein. But you could just as easily make them the main portion of your meal, especially warranted on a cold winter's day!

EASIEST POTATO ROSTI

No egg needed to bind this potato! No flour! No par-cooking! This is supreme minimalism with a purpose. Sometimes we overcomplicate things, don't we? Or maybe that's just me. This recipe requires a hot nonstick pan and a little focus. Can you dress up this potato cake? Yes! I suggest topping it with smoked salmon or smashed avocado or Greek yogurt with smoked pimento—all delicious choices.

1 large russet potato, peeled

2 tablespoons sliced fresh chives or scallions

3 tablespoons ghee

Salt and ground white pepper

Flaky sea salt, for finishing

Using the large holes of a standard box grater, shred the peeled potato into a medium-sized mixing bowl, then fold in the chives.

Heat the ghee in an 8- to 10-inch nonstick skillet over medium-high heat until it begins to smoke.

Add the shredded potato to the pan, being careful not to splatter the hot ghee. Using a rubber spatula, form the potato into a round cake, pressing down to help bind it together. Season lightly with salt and pepper.

Lower the heat to medium and cook the potato cake until golden brown around the edges, 5 to 7 minutes.

Using a large spatula and one smooth motion, flip the potato cake, season with a little more salt and pepper on this side, and cook until golden brown on the bottom, another 5 to 7 minutes.

Remove immediately to a plate lined with paper towels to absorb the excess ghee. Finish with some flaky salt and serve warm.

SWEET POTATO HASH BURRITOS

WITH EGGS & SOY CHORIZO

I met soyrizo a decade ago in Southern California. Maybe it had been around before, but I wasn't aware. We were introduced when the health movement met the breakfast burrito craze, and my mornings have never been the same. Soyrizo, a brand of soy-based chorizo, is a fun play on words (have I mentioned I like puns?). It's a plant-based alternative to chorizo, the popular Mexican pork sausage. The natural sweetness of the sweet potato is the perfect match for the spicy kick of the chorizo in this recipe. You could just as easily serve this hash as a side dish, but when wrapped up in a tortilla, it's a perfect breakfast or lunch.

FOR THE HASH

1 tablespoon olive oil

1 large sweet potato, peeled and diced

1 tablespoon finely diced yellow onions

1 clove garlic, smashed with the side of a knife

¼ teaspoon salt

Pinch of freshly ground black pepper

1 teaspoon ground cumin

8 ounces soy chorizo, removed from casing and crumbled

1 tablespoon tomato paste

2 tablespoons sliced scallions

2 tablespoons chopped fresh cilantro

A squeeze of lime juice

FOR THE BURRITOS

1 teaspoon ghee or unsalted butter

3 large eggs

Pinch of salt

Pinch of freshly ground black pepper

2 burrito-sized grain-free tortillas (see Notes)

½ cup diced avocado

½ cup Cotija cheese crumbles (see Notes)

Leaves from 3 sprigs fresh cilantro

2 tablespoons plain Greek yogurt

A few splashes of hot sauce (optional)

TO MAKE THE HASH:

In a sauté pan or large cast-iron skillet, heat the olive oil over medium heat. Add the sweet potato and cook for a few minutes, until it starts to take on a little color. Then add the onions, garlic, salt, pepper, and cumin and cook for another minute, or until the onions are translucent.

Add the soy chorizo and tomato paste and cook, stirring occasionally, until heated through, about 5 minutes, being careful not to cream the potatoes.

When the sweet potatoes are tender, add the scallions, cilantro, and lime juice. Stir and remove the hash from the pan.

TO MAKE THE BURRITOS:

In the same pan, melt the ghee over medium-high heat. Whisk the eggs, salt, and pepper until frothy. Pour the egg mixture into the pan and use a rubber spatula to stir and scrape up any loose bits of hash remaining on the bottom of the pan. (See Notes.)

Once large curds begin to form, shut off the heat but leave the eggs in the pan, turning until they are set to your preference. Remove the eggs from the pan.

Roll the tortillas in a damp paper towel and microwave for 30 seconds to soften them. Lay the tortillas on a flat surface and divide the hash, eggs, avocado, cheese, cilantro, and yogurt evenly between them, layering them in the center of each tortilla. Season with hot sauce, if desired, then roll up burrito-style and serve.

NOTES

Some grain-free tortillas need to be cooked before they can be eaten; if using this kind, be sure to cook them, following the package instructions for proper cooking technique, before assembling the burritos.

Cotija is a wonderful salty cow's milk cheese that is used predominantly in Mexican cuisine. If you have trouble sourcing it, feta is a worthy alternative.

When it comes to reusing pans, I don't mind the discoloration that happens because it's also layering flavor and saving the dishwasher a little time and effort too. If none of this appeals to you, feel free to swap out the pan for a clean one.

POMMES ANNA

OPTION

I made this dish once after returning from a Christmas vacation. On a whim, we filmed the process for TikTok. It got three million views in a few days. That's how much people love potatoes! You'll likely see this dish on the menu of any French chef who is worth their salt. *Pomme* is short for the French term for potato, *pomme de terre*, but don't let the name scare you. Yes, it's more glamorous than hash browns, but it has those familiar crisped brown edges that only a potato can give. You could serve this latke-style with some applesauce and sour cream or eat it out of hand like a giant potato chip. Ooh, now that I say potato chip, some crème fraîche and caviar wouldn't be a bad topping, either.

3 large Yukon Gold or russet potatoes (about 2 pounds), scrubbed

Ghee or clarified butter, for the pan

1 sprig fresh thyme or rosemary

Pinch of salt

Pinch of ground white pepper

NOTES

This is a lighter, more delicate approach to the traditional Pommes Anna, as it is a single layer instead of numerous layers of potato and butter. You still get the benefit of the buttery crisp edges but not the full caloric load of the original.

To make this recipe dairy free, use ghee rather than clarified butter.

Using a mandoline, shave the potatoes into thin coins. (If you don't have a mandoline, then do your best with a sharp knife.)

In a medium-sized nonstick skillet over high heat, melt enough ghee so that it comes ⅛ inch up the side of the pan. (Depending on the exact size of your pan, you'll likely need about 2 tablespoons.) Heat until just smoking. Swirl the thyme sprig in the ghee for a few moments to "scent" the ghee. Remove the thyme and set aside.

Start to add the potato coins in an overlapping pattern, beginning in the center of the pan and allowing each slice to cover about one-quarter of the adjacent coin. Continue overlapping the slices to form a concentric circle that covers the bottom of the skillet, but stop short of the edge of the pan by about ½ inch. (Leaving a bit of space around the edge will make flipping easier.) Season the potatoes with the salt and pepper. Reduce the heat to medium-low.

After 5 to 7 minutes, when the potatoes are light (not dark) brown on the edges, flip the whole circle using a large spatula and one smooth motion; it will be in one piece as the potatoes will have stuck together. Cook until golden brown and crispy on the other side, another 5 minutes or so.

Set the potatoes on a plate lined with paper towels to absorb some of the excess ghee. Garnish with the reserved thyme sprig and serve immediately.

BAKED SWEET POTATO FRIES
WITH GARLIC MAYO

Fries are my kryptonite, no doubt, and I'll be real here, there is no real healthy swap for them. Frying potatoes in hot oil is the only way to achieve that texture, although an air fryer gets close. However, this recipe for baked fries can satisfy that fry craving a little bit, and without all of the unhealthy parts. I've paired the fries with a simple homemade mayonnaise, an easy dish that just needs to be in your repertoire. As a professional chef, I often take for granted the things I learned early in my career, but the straightforward technique for making mayonnaise, a true mother sauce, always blows people's minds and brings me back to the foundation of cooking.

2 large sweet potatoes, cleaned and cut into ¾-inch-thick sticks

2 tablespoons olive oil

Salt

1 tablespoon chopped fresh parsley, for garnish

FOR THE GARLIC MAYO
(Makes 1½ cups)

1 large egg yolk

1 to 2 cloves garlic, minced

1 teaspoon prepared yellow mustard

Pinch of salt

1 cup avocado oil or extra-virgin olive oil

1½ teaspoons fresh lemon juice

1 to 2 teaspoons water (if needed)

1 teaspoon honey or agave nectar (optional)

Preheat the oven to 375°F. Line a sheet pan with aluminum foil.

Put the sweet potato sticks in a large mixing bowl and add the olive oil. Toss to coat the potatoes evenly.

Spread out the sweet potato sticks on the prepared pan so none are touching. Season generously with salt.

Bake the fries until lightly golden brown and crispy on the outside and tender on the inside, about 45 minutes. Flip the fries over about halfway through the cooking time.

While the sweet potatoes are baking, make the garlic mayo: Put the egg yolk, garlic, mustard, and salt in a medium-sized glass mixing bowl and slowly whisk in the oil until emulsified. Stir in the lemon juice. If the emulsion is too thick, whisk in a splash of water. Add the honey here too if you are so inclined. We like honey to offset the bitterness of a really good olive oil in this sauce; if using avocado oil, the added sweetness won't be needed.

Garnish the fries with the parsley and serve with the garlic mayo. Any leftover mayo will keep in the fridge for up to 2 weeks.

POTATOSTONES

(POTATO TOSTONES)

Sure, you can call these smashed potatoes or smashies, but I love a perfect phonetically similar food pun, and this fits the bill. Cooking the potatoes twice is very similar to the process for making tostones from plantains, which makes this dad joke really, really clever... These are delicious with chimichurri (page 40).

1 pound baby potatoes, any color

Salt

2 tablespoons ghee

1 tablespoon unsalted butter (see Note)

4 sprigs fresh thyme

Place the potatoes in a large pot of cold water with a small handful of salt. Bring to a boil and cook until the potatoes are tender, about 15 minutes. Drain the potatoes and then chill them for at least 30 minutes; longer is fine.

Using the flat side of a chef's knife, smash the chilled potatoes to about an inch thick without breaking them into pieces or mashing them completely.

Heat the ghee in a sauté pan over medium-high heat until lightly smoking. Add the flattened potatoes, working in batches and adding more ghee to the pan as needed. Season with more salt and cook until golden brown on both sides, about 5 minutes per side.

In the last few minutes of browning the potatoes, add the butter and thyme.

Remove the pan from the heat and lay the potatoes on a plate lined with paper towels to absorb the excess ghee and butter. Transfer to a tray or platter before serving.

NOTE

Adding butter toward the end of this recipe contributes flavor and depth, but if you added it at the beginning of the sear, the milk solids in it would burn. This also holds true when searing a steak or fish. Only add butter toward the end of the searing time and then baste away! Ghee is butter that has been heated to remove the milk solids, leaving just the liquid fats.

THANKSGIVING-STYLE BAKED SWEET POTATOES

OPTION

I made this recipe for a recent Thanksgiving dinner because I couldn't resist a healthy take on the classically over-sugared candied yam dish. When I was a kid, my mom would open up the can of syrupy yams and top them with marshmallows, maple syrup, and brown sugar, and...yeah, you get where I'm going—it's basically dessert. Sweet potato nectar, which you can find in most markets now, is the ultimate secret weapon for making a "candied" sweet potato or yam dish without refined sugars. Date syrup or maple syrup would be a fine swap. Not only are we happy with this dish filling in for the cloyingly sweet classic on our holiday table, but we much prefer it.

4 large sweet potatoes, peeled and cut into 2-inch-thick rounds

Salt

3 tablespoons sweet potato nectar

1 teaspoon white truffle oil (optional)

3 tablespoons unsalted butter

FOR TOPPING

3 tablespoons Sprouted Walnuts (page 48) or roasted pecans, roughly chopped

2 tablespoons pomegranate arils

2 tablespoons sliced scallions or fresh chives

Ground white pepper to taste

2 tablespoons grated Parmesan cheese (optional)

Preheat the oven to 350°F. Grease a 3-quart casserole dish with ghee or avocado oil.

Place the sweet potato rounds in a large pot of cold water with a small handful of salt. Bring to a boil, then lower the heat and simmer until the potatoes are halfway cooked, 10 to 15 minutes. The potatoes should be able to be pierced with a knife but still have a firm center.

Drain the sweet potatoes and arrange them in the greased casserole dish. Drizzle with the sweet potato nectar and the truffle oil, if using, then dot with the butter. Bake uncovered for 30 minutes, until the potatoes are fork-tender.

Remove from the oven and top with the nuts, pomegranate arils, scallions, pepper, and, if desired, the Parmesan cheese.

NOTE

The truffle oil and Parmesan are optional in this recipe, but using both brings an elevated, mature flavor profile to the dish and plays well off the sweet starchiness of the potatoes. Omit the Parmesan to make this recipe vegetarian.

MASHED RUTABAGA

OPTION   OPTION

You've seen rutabaga before. In fact, I guarantee you've walked by it thousands of times in grocery stores. It's a stubby root vegetable with a yellowish-brown waxy exterior. It's usually right next to those turnips you've been ignoring too. Grab a couple on your next shop and give this recipe a whirl. The more I make mashed rutabaga, a holiday tradition from Jazmin's side of the family (I'm very jealous I can't take credit for it), the more I don't even want to add butter. You can, and I usually still do for the extra richness it provides, but this recipe is super simple and delicious either way. If you want to add some chopped fresh parsley or sage to the mash for a holiday vibe, that's great as well.

3 to 4 large rutabaga (aka yellow turnips) (about 2 pounds)

Salt

2 to 4 tablespoons cold unsalted butter, according to taste

Ground white or black pepper

Using a paring knife, peel the rutabaga to remove the waxy skin and reveal the yellow flesh. Roughly chop the peeled rutabaga.

Put the rutabaga in a large saucepan and cover with cold water. Add a small handful of salt and boil until tender; an inserted knife tip should easily slide out of a cooked piece.

Drain the rutabaga and return it to the pan. Mash well with a potato masher or large fork until it looks like mashed potatoes.

Toss in the butter, season with some pepper and a little more salt, and continue mashing until the butter becomes one with the rutabaga. Serve warm.

NOTE
To make this dish dairy free and vegan, omit the butter.

A SIMPLE ROASTED CHICKEN

WITH VEGETABLES FROM THE FRIDGE

OPTION

As we've made clear from the beginning of this book, we aren't vegetarians. Well, Jazmin has been for stretches of time, but I love cooking and eating meat. Has the classic roasted chicken been over-romanticized? It's debatable. But you'd lose the debate if you took that side. It's my favorite aroma, a smell that welcomes you home after a long day. It might even make a good candle scent, although you'd be tempted to eat the candle, which sounds like a course off a tasting menu at an avant-garde restaurant run by a genius chef (don't tell anyone where you heard about edible chicken candles first). This recipe, of course, is more crowd-pleasing than cutting-edge, so everyone will be happy to dig in. It's a meal you can make happen even if you are picking up your bird on the way home from work. You'll need an hour and fifteen minutes and a few vegetables from the fridge for a one-"pan" meal. The drippings in the pan are used like liquid gold to start a nice sauce to accompany the meal.

1 roasting-sized chicken (about 3½ pounds)

3 tablespoons ghee, room temperature

2 tablespoons salt

1 tablespoon ground white pepper

1½ teaspoons granulated garlic

5 small carrots (marker-sized or slightly larger), peeled or washed

1 medium yellow onion, cut into quarters

1 (1½-pound) bag baby potatoes (about 2 cups)

2 sprigs fresh thyme

2 tablespoons chopped fresh parsley

2 lemon wedges

FOR THE PAN SAUCE

Drippings from the roasting pan

1 tablespoon balsamic vinegar

1 tablespoon date syrup or maple syrup (optional; see Notes)

1 teaspoon prepared yellow mustard

½ teaspoon coconut aminos or soy sauce

Preheat the oven to 450°F.

Rinse the chicken and pat dry with a towel. Remove the innards, reserving the neck for the pan and discarding the rest. Rub the ghee all over the bird and season it with the salt, pepper, and granulated garlic.

Place the vegetables in a roasting pan and lay the chicken, breast side up, on top of them. (If you prefer to use a rack, place the chicken on the rack in the pan and spread the vegetables around the chicken.) Add the reserved neck to the pan as well. Roast uncovered for 25 minutes.

Turn the oven temperature down to 350°F. Place one sprig of thyme on the chicken and the other on the vegetables and continue roasting for 30 minutes, or until a meat thermometer registers a minimum of 165°F when inserted into the thickest part of the thigh. This will give you a just-cooked and ultra-juicy bird. Add another 15 minutes if you prefer it a little crispier and more well-done around the thighs. Personally, I err for group satisfaction and like the extra 15 minutes, which will take the internal temperature of the thigh to 175°F.

Remove the bird from the pan and place on a flat carving surface to rest for 15 minutes.

Spoon the vegetables into a large serving bowl, leaving the drippings and chicken neck in the roasting pan. Toss with the parsley for family-style serving. Squeeze the lemon wedges over the vegetables and sprinkle with salt.

To make the pan sauce, set the roasting pan on the stovetop over low heat and add the vinegar to the drippings while scraping the bottom of the pan with a wooden spoon. Remove and discard the neck. Turn off the heat and whisk in the syrup (if using), mustard, and coconut aminos. Voilà! Sauce!

Carve the bird and spoon the sauce over the chicken. Serve with the roasted vegetables.

NOTES

The tiny bit of added syrup in the pan sauce balances the acidity and rounds out the richness. Taste the sauce before adding it to determine if you feel it's needed.

To make this recipe gluten free, use coconut aminos rather than soy sauce in the pan sauce.

GREENS

I remember when "eating your greens" meant mushy, grayish cut green beans from a can. I remember thinking collards were only for New Year's Day. I remember when there was only Caesar salad, not kale Caesar salad (see page 132). We have come a long way since then, and greens have too. The types and colors of greens available can be astounding at your local grocer and even more so at a farmers' market. Chard, kale, collards, broccoli greens, beet greens—there are so many choices. Have you tried broccoli greens? No!? Trust us, they're delicious if you can find them, and if not, there's bound to be plenty of other options at a market near you. The recipes in this chapter may call for a certain green, but if the whim strikes, you can usually replace it with another green of your choice. Many of them function the same way in a recipe, although the taste and texture do vary a bit.

As parents, we love greens as a sly additive to bulk up the health quotient of recipes. We toss chopped kale or spinach into pasta dishes like Bolognese, and into soups and smoothies. If you start them young enough, kids won't even ask why there are green bits in the pasta sauce when they're teenagers. And while it can be hard to hide greens in a smoothie, our challenge is to make a tasty kid-approved smoothie that is also GREEN. It can be done! Jazmin's Green Smoothie recipe on page 150 is proof of that.

When we started writing this book, some chapters were easier to develop than others. We tried to provide recipes in each chapter for every meal period, and that was not always a simple task. But for Greens, it was. Greens can easily be in salads, so lunch is covered, but their superpower is that they can be added to lots of dishes without compromising flavor or authenticity. Toss them in with a tomato sauce or a pesto pasta dish and no one complains. They easily melt into a soup and provide texture and nuance. And sautéed greens are happy to be a bed for a nice piece of fish or some poached breakfast eggs. We'll bet that you already have a few recipes that you're thinking could benefit from a handful of spinach or kale tossed in, and that's the health-forward progress we are looking for that can make a big nutritional difference in your day.

From a nutrition standpoint, greens steal the show. Because they are high in vitamins and minerals but low in calories, you can eat loads of them and really dial up the health benefits. If it's green (or sometimes even purple), you're guaranteed to get your money's worth in the nutrition category. There are also too many greens and too many ways to prepare them to say categorically that you don't like greens. If you don't love mustard greens because they can be a tad bitter and biting, swap them out for the smooth verdancy of spinach. Also, if you handle them appropriately, you can eat greens raw, cooked, blended, or baked. The opportunities are abundant, plus the growing seasons are long. This might be the most powerful section in a cookbook geared toward healthier eating. So, don't just flip casually past this chapter. Dig in!

A NICE SPINACH SALAD

WITH SPROUTED WALNUTS & DRIED MULBERRIES

OPTION   OPTION

The most interesting thing about this salad is the mulberries—a healthier, tastier version of dried sweetened cranberries. White mulberries are a lovely superfood that have high levels of iron, vitamin C, and antioxidants. You can find this superberry in its dried form in the bulk bins at health food stores near the other dried fruits or online. Otherwise, this is a gratifying spinach salad with a tasty vinaigrette, perfect for a lunch for two.

FOR THE DRESSING

(Makes about ½ cup)

⅓ cup extra-virgin olive oil

2 tablespoons red wine vinegar or apple cider vinegar

2 teaspoons Dijon mustard

1 teaspoon honey or other liquid sweetener of choice

1 clove garlic, minced

⅛ teaspoon salt

⅛ teaspoon freshly ground black pepper

10 ounces baby spinach, rinsed and dried

½ cup Sprouted Walnuts (page 48), chopped

¼ cup dried white mulberries

¼ cup crumbled fresh (soft) goat cheese (optional)

Put all of the ingredients for the dressing in a glass jar with a well-fitting lid and shake vigorously until emulsified. Refrigerate to chill slightly, up to an hour. Any leftover dressing can be stored in the refrigerator for up to 3 days.

Place the spinach in a large salad bowl. Add the remaining salad ingredients and half of the dressing and toss. Drizzle with more dressing, if desired, and serve.

NOTE
To make this recipe dairy free, omit the goat cheese.
To make it vegan, also use a vegan liquid sweetener, such as date syrup.

WAY BETTER COLESLAW

When you challenge yourself to follow a new nutritional plan, sometimes there is one thing that absolutely saves your willpower and makes the day a little better. This recipe was that thing for Jazmin the last time we did a six-week cleanse. It has way less mayonnaise than most prepared coleslaws, no added sugar, and a touch of protein from the addition of Greek yogurt. It's crunchy and piquant, and you can eat it as is, use it as a topping for chili, or wrap it up in a corn tortilla with some sliced avocado. We have found many different uses for this quick salad, and I bet you will too.

¼ cup avocado oil mayonnaise

¼ cup plain Greek yogurt

1 tablespoon apple cider vinegar

1 teaspoon Dijon mustard

¼ teaspoon whole-grain mustard

⅛ teaspoon salt

A couple grinds of black pepper

1 scallion, thinly sliced

1 tablespoon chopped fresh parsley or cilantro (leaves and stems)

¼ teaspoon dried dill weed

1 large carrot, peeled and julienned

½ head green cabbage, shredded

In a large mixing bowl, whisk together the mayo, yogurt, vinegar, mustards, salt, and pepper.

Fold in the scallion, parsley, and dill and incorporate well.

Add the carrot and cabbage to the dressing and turn until evenly coated. Chill the slaw before serving if you have time. It can be kept in an airtight container in the refrigerator for up to 5 days.

EVERYDAY KALE SALAD
WITH AVOCADO & PINE NUTS

This salad is about as clean as you can get. Smashed avocado combines with the juice of a lemon and a little olive oil for the dressing. The pine nuts are optional; you can omit them or substitute any type of nut. I've also been known to add some pickled red onion if I have it on hand. Another note: Massaging kale may seem like a Gen-Zer's request, but it came from Jazmin directly, and I'm a convert to the technique because of this recipe. Serve this salad with anything, to anyone, at any time.

2 avocados

Juice of 1 lemon

2 tablespoons extra-virgin olive oil

Salt and pepper

16 ounces kale, ribs removed, sliced into thin ribbons

¼ cup toasted pine nuts, for topping

Peel and pit the avocados. Put one avocado in a large salad bowl, preferably a wooden one. Dice the other avocado and set aside.

Smash the avocado in the bowl with the lemon juice, then swirl in the olive oil, a little salt, and a few grinds of pepper. Whisk until you get a nice emulsion that resembles salad dressing.

Add the kale and mix and massage with your hands for a few minutes to break down some of the cell structure of the hearty green while incorporating the dressing fully. (If you've ever had a kale salad and felt like you had to chew it forever, this step was skipped...don't skip this step.)

Top with the diced avocado and toasted pine nuts and serve.

SPINACH ARTICHOKE DIP

OPTION   OPTION

The ubiquitous and crave-worthy spinach artichoke dip. You can scoff at it, make fun of your aunt who uses a French onion soup flavor packet in her version (delicious, but definitely salty and overprocessed), but I dare you to pass up a bowl at a party. Why not embrace your instinct and make some dip of your own while being mindful of how much dairy and fat you put in it? As in the Parsnip Creamed Spinach recipe on page 146, you capture the same creaminess that milk, flour, and butter bring to a recipe by macerating a complementary-flavored vegetable into the dish. Here, it's obviously artichoke hearts that you can find in a jar or can in most markets. Serve with tortilla chips, baked plantain chips, warm tortillas, or crudités.

1 pound baby spinach

½ cup plain unsweetened coconut milk

2 cups artichoke hearts, drained and roughly chopped

1 tablespoon Italian seasoning

½ teaspoon salt

¼ teaspoon freshly ground black pepper

½ cup crumbled feta cheese or plant-based feta

¼ cup shredded part-skim mozzarella cheese or vegan mozzarella shreds

3 tablespoons finely diced canned water chestnuts

Rinse and pat dry the spinach. Buzz the spinach in a food processor until it reaches pesto consistency—a very fine chop but not liquefied.

Warm the coconut milk in a large saucepan over medium heat. Add the chopped artichoke hearts to the pan, mashing them further with a wooden spoon.

Add the seasonings and chopped spinach and cook uncovered for a few minutes, until the spinach is tender and the mixture begins to thicken.

Remove from the heat and, while still warm, stir in the cheeses and water chestnuts. Serve warm.

NOTE
To make this recipe dairy free and vegan, use plant-based cheeses.

CALDO VERDE
(GREEN SOUP)

OPTION

One day maybe I'll write a book on soups, because I could easily live on them. This is a version of a Portuguese classic—hearty and filling. I add white beans to up the protein and make it even more nutritionally dense. I love to use meat or chicken stock here, but substituting vegetable stock and adding a dash of coconut aminos will work as well. Use a plant-based sausage, and you have yourself a bowl of vegan comfort.

¼ **cup diced yellow onions**

¼ **cup diced carrots**

3 tablespoons minced garlic

1 tablespoon olive oil

8 ounces fresh Mexican-style chorizo or andouille sausage (meat- or plant-based)

1 teaspoon Cajun seasoning blend

1 teaspoon smoked paprika

2 quarts beef, chicken, or vegetable stock

Splash of coconut aminos (if using vegetable stock)

16 ounces kale and/or collard greens, ribs removed, finely sliced

2 medium Yukon Gold potatoes, diced

1 (15-ounce) can white beans, drained and rinsed

Salt and pepper

Hot pepper vinegar, for serving

In a soup pot, cook the onions, carrots, and garlic in the olive oil over medium heat for a few minutes, until everything starts to soften.

If using chorizo, crumble the sausage into the soup pot. If using andouille, cut the links into 1-inch slices before dropping them into the pot. Add the spices and cook for a few more minutes, until you've gotten a nice sear on the sausage.

Add the stock and scrape any cooked bits off the bottom of the pot with a wooden spoon while stirring. Add the coconut aminos (if using), kale, potatoes, and beans and stir to incorporate. Simmer uncovered for 30 minutes, or until the potatoes are fork-tender.

Taste and adjust the seasoning with salt and pepper. Serve with pepper vinegar on the side.

NOTE
To make this recipe vegan, use a plant-based sausage and vegetable stock.

SHAVED KALE SALAD

WITH COCONUT CASHEW 'CAESAR' DRESSING

OPTION

Eat and cook what you like. I like Caesar salad. Here's a somewhat tropical take on the dressing that I serve at one of my restaurants, Four Flamingos in Orlando, Florida. Coconut milk and cashews replace the mayo and punch up both the flavor and the nutrition. Cashews have a great richness and creaminess, making them a more than dependable replacement for milk or cheese in recipes. They do, however, add a good bit of fat and calories, so use them judiciously. Here I use the cashews as a complement, enriching the dressing but allowing the coconut to remain the star ingredient. Toss some grilled chicken on this salad and make it a lunch you'd get at a fancy spa!

FOR THE DRESSING
(Makes roughly 1½ cups)

1 cup plain unsweetened coconut milk

¼ cup Cashew Cheese Spread (page 46)

¼ cup grated Parmesan cheese or plant-based parmesan

2 tablespoons roughly chopped garlic

1 rounded tablespoon capers, drained

1 teaspoon anchovy paste, or 1 anchovy (packed in oil), drained and roughly chopped

Juice of ½ lemon

½ teaspoon coconut aminos

¼ teaspoon salt

A few grinds of black pepper

Juice of ½ lemon

2 teaspoons olive oil

3 bunches kale, ribs removed, sliced into very thin strips (almost shredded) (about 1 quart)

½ cup Coconut Cashew Caesar Dressing (from left), plus more if desired

½ cup store-bought plantain croutons or lightly crushed plantain chips, for topping

Shredded Parmesan cheese, for topping (optional)

Put all of the ingredients for the dressing in a blender and blend until smooth. Taste and adjust the salt and pepper as needed. Store the leftover dressing in the refrigerator for up to 10 days.

In a large mixing bowl, whisk together the lemon juice and olive oil until just emulsified. Add the kale and massage a bit with your hands to disperse the lemony olive oil and tenderize the kale.

Add the dressing and toss to combine. I like my kale salad pretty heavily dressed; you can adjust the amount of dressing according to your taste.

Top with the plantain croutons or chips and some Parmesan cheese, if desired.

NOTE
To make this recipe dairy free, use plant-based parmesan.

BROCCOLI TOP "PESTO"

WITH KALE & WHOLE-WHEAT SPAGHETTI

OPTION OPTION OPTION

This recipe is a Blais family classic. I absolutely adore pumping up this "pesto" with lots of minced broccoli and kale. It is closer to a traditional pesto than you might think, especially because of the pine nuts and Parmesan, and the dish definitely hearkens to a pesto-style pasta dish. It's also flush with superfoods, providing vitamins C and K1 along with potassium and folate. And it's a great way to slip in lots of vegetables for your kids or family and friends who may not like green vegetables but will devour this friendly pasta bowl.

1 pound whole-wheat or gluten-free spaghetti

1 medium head broccoli

2 tablespoons minced garlic

½ teaspoon Calabrian chili oil or red pepper flakes

2 tablespoons olive oil

2 cups destemmed and minced or pulverized kale leaves

½ cup pine nuts

1½ cups fresh basil leaves, minced

3 tablespoons grated Parmesan cheese, or 1 tablespoon nutritional yeast

Juice of ½ lemon

Salt and pepper

Chopped Calabrian chili peppers (packed in oil) or red pepper flakes, for serving

Cook the spaghetti per the package instructions for al dente. Reserve ¼ cup of the pasta water, then drain the pasta. Do not rinse the pasta.

Using a sharp knife, shave the greenest parts of the frilly tops off the broccoli, leaving the stems. You want about 1 cup of shaved broccoli tops.

In a sauté pan big enough for all of the pasta, warm the garlic and chili oil in the olive oil over medium heat until the garlic is fragrant.

Add the kale, broccoli tops, and pine nuts to the pan and cook, stirring occasionally, for 2 to 3 minutes, until the kale has softened but everything is still green and bright.

Add the basil, Parmesan (if using), lemon juice, and reserved pasta water. Cook briefly to combine the flavors, then season with salt and pepper to taste.

Add the cooked pasta to the pan, tossing gently to coat in the sauce. Remove from the heat and turn the pasta a few more times to fully incorporate the sauce.

Serve with a scattering of chopped Calabrian chilies or a few red pepper flakes on top.

Track down a jar of Calabrian chilies in oil and you'll find uses for them (both the peppers and the oil) all the time! Check your local specialty store or order them online.

To make this recipe dairy free and vegan, use nutritional yeast rather than Parmesan cheese. To make it gluten free, use a gluten-free spaghetti.

MELTING CABBAGE

WITH GOOD BUTTER, PICKLING SPICES & DILL

Is cabbage intimidating? Does it have a bad publicist? No and maybe. You usually only see a run on green cabbage around Saint Patrick's Day, or find cabbage chopped into slaw at barbecues. But cabbage is one of my favorites in the vegetable world for its savory funk and silky texture when steamed like this in a little water and some good-quality butter. This recipe is a perfect vegetarian swap for a Saint Patrick's Day feast because the pickling spices give the illusion of corned beef, but I have a feeling you'll be making this dish more than once a year.

1 medium head green cabbage, quartered with the core intact

¾ cup water

2 tablespoons unsalted butter

1 tablespoon pickling spices

1½ teaspoons salt (if there is no salt in the pickling spices)

2 tablespoons roughly chopped fresh dill

Flaky sea salt, for finishing

In a medium-sized saucepot with a lid, combine the cabbage, water, butter, pickling spices, and salt, if using. Cover and simmer over medium heat for 30 minutes, or until the cabbage is fork-tender.

Remove the lid and glaze the cabbage with the reduced liquid, spooning the buttery goodness over the cabbage quarters.

To serve, transfer the cabbage to a shallow serving bowl, then sprinkle on the dill and a little flaky salt.

CRISPY BRUSSELS SPROUTS

WITH CHILI, LIME & COCONUT SUGAR

A new classic for sure. Frying and charring vegetables until they are almost burnt brings out new depths of flavor. Many cultures have known this for ages, but American restaurants only caught on in the last decade or so. Who hasn't seen a crispy Brussels dish at their neighborhood spot? To keep this version healthier, I'm not frying but rather roasting the Brussels sprouts in high heat and being mindful of the type of sugar used in the dressing. Spicy, sweet, salty, and funky, this dish, or a variation of it, can be found at many of my establishments and even on our family's Thanksgiving table from time to time.

2 tablespoons finely diced pancetta

12 ounces Brussels sprouts, bottoms trimmed, cut in half

Salt and pepper

1½ teaspoons olive oil

1 tablespoon fish sauce

1 tablespoon lime juice

1½ teaspoons coconut sugar or honey

2 tablespoons chopped fresh cilantro

1 Thai chili pepper (aka bird's eye chili), seeded and sliced (see Note)

1½ tablespoons sliced scallions

Preheat the oven to 400°F. Line a sheet pan with aluminum foil.

In a small skillet over medium heat, cook the pancetta until crispy, 5 to 7 minutes. Remove the pancetta to a paper towel to absorb the excess grease and set aside.

Place the halved Brussels sprouts on the prepared sheet pan, season generously with salt and pepper, and drizzle with the olive oil. Roast until browned and crispy, about 30 minutes, giving the pan a shake about halfway through to toss the sprouts and allow them to cook on the other side. Some of the leaves will get really crispy and charred, and that's OK!

Meanwhile, make the dressing: In a small mixing bowl, whisk together the fish sauce, lime juice, sugar, cilantro, chili, and scallions.

When the Brussels are cooked, transfer them to a serving bowl and toss with the dressing. Top with the crispy pancetta and serve.

NOTE
If you have trouble sourcing a Thai chili pepper, a Serrano chili will substitute nicely.

SAUTÉED SPINACH

WITH BLACK GARLIC & LEMON

This is maybe the simplest recipe in the book, and possibly the first thing I ever cooked in a restaurant. It's a perfect side for any protein, and easily customizable. I love taking simple dishes and adding a bit of nuance to them: here, mellow aged black garlic is what sets this preparation apart. But if you can't find black garlic, pickled, smoked, roasted, or minced fresh garlic will do. Replace the lemon with grapefruit or other citrus, but whatever you do, resist the urge to add liquid to the pan. The spinach has enough natural liquid content and will release it when heated. No one wants soggy sautéed spinach!

1½ teaspoons olive oil

24 ounces baby spinach

3 cloves black garlic, smashed with the side of a knife (see Note)

½ teaspoon grated lemon zest

Squeeze of lemon juice

Pinch of salt

Grind or two of black pepper

Heat the olive oil in a sauté pan over medium heat. Add the spinach and smashed black garlic and cook for 2 minutes maximum, until just wilted, then remove the spinach to a serving bowl.

Add the lemon zest, juice, salt, and pepper and stir to combine. Serve warm.

NOTE

Black garlic is aged garlic with a slightly sweeter taste than the raw form. It's usually found in a can or jar.

BRAISED HOLIDAY GREENS

OPTION

You don't have to wait for the holidays to cook this dish. As a matter of fact, any Tuesday will do. This is a classic braised greens dish that uses "uncured" bacon, which means it's cured but with naturally sourced nitrites from vegetables. To me, it tastes a little less salty. Feel free to omit the bacon altogether and add a little smoked paprika for that smoky flavor, or replace the bacon with pancetta or prosciutto or even a chopped-up vegan hot dog if that's what you're working with. That's what real cooking is all about: no ingredient roadblocks, only answers to the question of how to create something delicious using what you have on hand.

3 bunches collard greens, kale, spinach, or Swiss chard

½ cup chopped uncured bacon

¼ cup finely diced yellow onions

2 tablespoons sliced garlic

½ teaspoon Calabrian chili oil or red pepper flakes

1 to 2 tablespoons water, if needed (see Notes)

1 teaspoon salt

½ teaspoon freshly ground black pepper

Grated zest of 1 lemon

Juice of ½ lemon

Rinse the greens thoroughly and pat dry. Remove the ribs and chop the leaves into bite-sized pieces.

In a large pot over low heat, cook the bacon for about 3 minutes, until the fat starts to render.

Add the onions, garlic, and chili oil and sauté for 2 more minutes, until the onions have softened and the mixture is fragrant.

Add the greens and turn to coat in the bacon drippings. Cook uncovered, turning the contents of the pot occasionally to keep the onions and garlic from browning, for another 8 to 10 minutes for collards or kale or 3 to 4 minutes for spinach or Swiss chard. If needed, add a tablespoon or two of water to the pot to assist in braising. When done, the greens should be wilted but still vibrantly colored.

Season with the salt, pepper, lemon zest, and juice. Taste and adjust the seasoning as necessary.

NOTES

Depending on the greens you choose, you may not need water for this recipe; some types release plenty of liquid for braising once heated. Sometimes kale and collards do benefit from the addition of a splash of water to avoid browning.

To make this recipe vegan, replace the bacon with 2 teaspoons of smoked paprika.

PARSNIP CREAMED SPINACH

There's a lot to love about this dish, from the method you use to get that frozen spinach texture using fresh spinach to the added culinary perfume you get from the parsnips and nutmeg. But what we truly adore is that this is both a restaurant dish and a healthy version of a classic. You'll use TWO FULL BAGS of spinach, around 2 quarts packed by volume, for just four servings. Surely you've seen the memes about how ridiculously spinach cooks down, but it means you're getting all that nutrition in just a few power-packed bites. You can enjoy the classics, be creative, and be healthy all at the same time, which is the point of this book, isn't it?! *[Checks notes.]* Yes, yes it is. Serve as a side for a grilled steak or any simply grilled protein.

1 large parsnip, peeled and sliced into thin rounds

1 cup plain unsweetened coconut milk

¼ teaspoon salt

Small pinch of ground white pepper

Dash of freshly grated nutmeg or ground nutmeg

1 pound baby spinach

1½ teaspoons olive oil

1½ teaspoons finely diced shallot or white onion

½ teaspoon grated lemon zest

In a large saucepan over medium-low heat, cook the parsnip in the coconut milk with the salt, pepper, and nutmeg until tender, about 15 minutes.

Transfer the contents of the pan to a blender and blend until smooth.

Rinse and pat dry the spinach, then place in a food processor and buzz until the spinach is finely chopped. (Think spinach dip texture here.)

Heat the olive oil in a sauté pan over medium heat. Once warm, add the shallot and cook until fragrant and translucent, about 2 minutes.

Add the chopped spinach and cook, tossing frequently, until wilted, 1 to 2 minutes.

Add the parsnip mixture and lemon zest, stirring to incorporate fully. Cook for another few moments to let the flavors meld, then remove from the heat and serve.

JAZMIN'S GREEN SMOOTHIE

OPTION

This is a green smoothie for people who don't like green juice (ahem...Jazmin). We prefer smoothies to juicing because they preserve all that great fiber in the whole fruit and/or vegetable.

1½ cups baby spinach

1 (3-inch) piece cucumber, roughly chopped

¼ cup chopped fresh pineapple

A few sprigs fresh parsley

¼ teaspoon peeled and grated fresh ginger (optional)

½ cup water

½ cup ice cubes

1 tablespoon flax seeds

1 tablespoon hemp seeds

1 scoop plain collagen powder (optional, see Note)

Place all of the ingredients in the order listed in a high-powered blender and blend until smooth.

Serve immediately or store in the refrigerator for up to 1 day.

NOTE

Collagen powder is a type of protein powder that replicates one of the most abundant types of protein in the human body. Adding it here increases the nutritional load of this smoothie. Drink it post-workout to help with recovery and muscle repair. To make this recipe vegan, omit the collagen.

CHOCOLATE ALMOND SMOOTHIE

Wait a second, chocolate...almond...but what about the greens? Well, they're hidden from the recipe title, just like they are in this delicious anytime smoothie. We like to use a simple plant-based protein powder with just a few ingredients and not a lot of added sugar (Four Sigmatic is the brand we prefer). Further, we amplify it with powdered almond butter to increase the available protein. This smoothie is a meal or a great post-workout fiber and protein bomb.

¾ cup plain unsweetened nondairy milk alternative of choice or water

1 cup ice cubes

1 frozen banana, cut into 3-inch segments

½ cup baby spinach

¼ cup cottage cheese

2½ tablespoons (1 heaping scoop) chocolate-flavored protein powder

1 tablespoon powdered almond butter

1 teaspoon MCT oil (see Note)

1 medjool date, pitted and roughly chopped

Place all of the ingredients in the order listed in a high-powered blender and blend until smooth. Serve immediately or store in the refrigerator for up to 1 day.

NOTE

If you've never used MCT oil before, it can be wise to start with a smaller amount and work up to the 1 teaspoon called for in this recipe. It has a laxative effect on some people.

SQUASH

As I'm writing this intro, there's a chill in the air at dawn and at dusk. Football is back on television, and stores are starting to showcase various pumpkin-flavored items, more and more every year. Yes! It's fall! After a long hot summer, there's nothing better than the color scheme shift from green and yellows to oranges and reds, both in the flora and foliage and in the vegetables growing and popping up at the market. Even now, in front of our local grocery stores, bins are filling up with pumpkins, squash, gourds, and flint corn in a gorgeous array of colors. Truly, "eating the rainbow" would be more difficult without the diverse hues of summer and fall squash varieties.

This chapter includes recipes for summer squashes and the harder, heartier fall and winter varietals. Both have their merits. Summer squashes are easy to grow, easy to cook or grill, and pleasing to the eye with their pops of verdant green and sunshine yellow. I can't look at a crookneck squash and not think succotash with some corn, broad beans, and tomatoes. It's like summer's greatest hits! Hard squash varietals, like acorn, butternut, kabocha, and, yes, even jack-o-lantern pumpkins are stalwarts in soups, salads, and purees. They bake and roast well and can serve as a main dish or side. Plus, let's not forget the gift that keeps on giving for hard squashes: their seeds. Scoop them out, rinse them, and roast them, and you have a superfood snack loaded with protein that boosts brain function, bone health, and muscle health.

All types of squash are nutritional superstars from blossom to seed. It's hard to find a category of produce with such range of flavors and uses that also packs so much of a vitamin and mineral punch. Squashes are high in vitamins A and C, the antioxidant power couple that fights inflammation and can boost your immune defenses as well. They are high in fiber, potassium, and magnesium too. Fiber is key here: we haven't talked about it much yet, but it's a vital addition to your diet as it can lower cholesterol, regulate blood sugar, improve your gut microbiome, and make you feel full and satiated after a meal. Fiber is a superhero! Fiber is the reason your doctor tells you to eat more plants. Fiber is critical to better health, and in the following pages, it's delicious as well. It is best sourced from natural sources like beans, whole grains, and, yes, vegetables.

BUTTERNUT SQUASH SOUP

OPTION   OPTION

As ubiquitous as pumpkin spiced lattes, butternut squash soup appearing on menus marks the arrival of autumn for me. Bad versions can be too creamy, dessert-like, and boring. The way to keep this soup exciting even outside the fall season is to mix up the liquid base and get creative with the toppings. Butternut squash or any of the hard fall squashes can be a blank canvas for a plethora of crunchy, spicy, or herbaceous garnishes.

1 large butternut squash (about 4 pounds)

2 tablespoons olive oil, divided

1 teaspoon kosher salt

¼ teaspoon ground white pepper

1 large white onion, diced

3 cloves garlic

1 (1-inch) piece fresh ginger, peeled and roughly chopped

2 cups vegetable stock

2 cups plain unsweetened almond, coconut, or walnut milk

2 tablespoons unsalted butter (optional; see Notes)

¼ cup chopped fresh cilantro, for garnish

SUGGESTED TOPPINGS

Chinese chili crisp (see Notes)

Pumpkin pie spice

Sprouted Walnuts (page 48) or chopped almonds

Diced apple

Sliced scallions

2 lime wedges

Preheat the oven to 350°F.

Line a sheet pan with aluminum foil. Cut the squash in half lengthwise and scoop out the seeds and ligneous fibers from the center. Rub each fleshy half with ½ tablespoon of olive oil and season with the salt and pepper.

Lay the squash halves flesh side down on the lined pan and roast until a knife slides easily into the thickest part of the squash, about 45 minutes. Allow to cool for 5 minutes, then scoop the flesh from the skin and set aside. Discard the skins.

Warm the remaining tablespoon of oil in a heavy-bottomed saucepot over medium heat. Add the onion, garlic, and ginger and cook for a few minutes, until fragrant. Transfer the roasted squash flesh to the pot along with the stock and milk. Stir to incorporate well, then simmer for 15 minutes, allowing the flavors to meld.

Remove the pot from the heat, add the butter, and stir until it has fully melted. Working in batches if needed, transfer the soup to a blender and purée until silky smooth.

Taste and adjust the seasoning with salt and pepper.

Ladle into bowls and garnish with the cilantro, along with chili crisp, pumpkin pie spice, nuts, apple, scallions, and/or a squeeze of lime.

NOTES

The butter adds a richness that balances this vegetable-based soup. However, it is optional, so if you wish to keep the soup dairy free and vegan, then omit the butter.

Chinese chili crisp is an on-trend sauce but not one without substance. A staple in the Chinese cuisine pantry, it features a base of chilies fried in oil with various crunchy mix-ins depending on the maker. It's part sauce, part crunchy topping, and all delicious. Momofuku makes a good one, as does Fly by Jing. It's readily available in grocery stores and online.

ZUCCHINI FRITTERS
WITH PARMESAN

OPTION

I worked on this dish with the American Heart Association, so you know it's heart healthy! I really enjoy challenging my professional acumen as a chef to provide tasty food that actual doctors will stamp as "healthy." We all know that if you add enough cream and butter, anything can be delicious, but here it's all about the zucchini, a little thyme, and a nice sear.

2 medium zucchinis, grated (about 3 cups)

¼ cup minced shallots

2 large eggs, lightly beaten

½ cup all-purpose gluten-free flour

¼ cup grated Parmesan cheese, or 2 tablespoons nutritional yeast

1½ teaspoons chopped fresh thyme

1 teaspoon baking powder

1 teaspoon salt

1 teaspoon freshly ground black pepper

Avocado oil, for the pan

FOR SERVING

¼ cup nonfat plain Greek yogurt (see Notes)

4 lemon wedges

In a large mixing bowl, stir together the zucchini, shallots, eggs, flour, Parmesan, thyme, baking powder, salt, and pepper until well combined.

In a large nonstick skillet, heat about 1 tablespoon of avocado oil over medium heat, swirling to coat the pan. Place four scant ¼-cup portions of the zucchini mixture in the skillet. Using the back of the measuring cup or a spoon, gently press down on the zucchini mixture, spreading it into rounds about ½ inch thick.

Cook until golden brown on both sides, 3 to 4 minutes per side. Transfer the fritters to a paper towel–lined plate. Repeat with the remaining zucchini mixture.

Let the fritters cool for 5 minutes. Just before serving, top each fritter with a dollop of yogurt and a squeeze of lemon.

NOTES

Using nonfat yogurt is what makes this recipe heart healthy; if this isn't a concern for you, use any type of plain Greek yogurt you like.

To make this recipe vegetarian, use nutritional yeast rather than Parmesan cheese.

SPAGHETTI SQUASH

WITH THE SIMPLEST TOMATO SAUCE

Many moons ago, I was an impudent young chef who loved a good pun (I've only recently shed the impudent part). I had a restaurant that served thirty-one courses, and one of the many bites was always an "impasta"—a dish designed to have the feel of pasta but not actually made of flour and water. This is notable because it was way back in the early 2000s before the gluten-free craze really took hold. Spaghetti squash is the original impasta. You simply shred the cooked squash with a fork, and you have what resembles an autumnal pasta dish with minimal effort and no gluten. Why didn't I take the easy route and use it instead of agar agar noodles?!

1 large spaghetti squash (about 2 pounds)

4 tablespoons olive oil, divided

Salt and pepper

2 cloves garlic, minced

1 large tomato, finely diced

1 tablespoon tomato paste

1 teaspoon dried oregano leaves

4 to 5 large fresh basil leaves, chopped

Preheat the oven to 350°F.

Cut the squash in half lengthwise. Scoop out the seeds and discard.

Using 2 tablespoons of the olive oil, grease a sheet pan or large baking dish. Sprinkle salt and pepper on the flesh of the squash and place the halves cut side down on the pan. Bake for 1 hour, or until the skin of the squash is soft to the touch and the flesh pulls away easily with a fork.

Using a fork, scrape the cooked flesh out of the skin using long strokes to preserve the integrity of the spaghetti "noodles."

In a sauté pan over medium heat, warm the remaining 2 tablespoons of olive oil. Add the garlic and cook, moving it around constantly to prevent it from browning, until fragrant, about 2 minutes. Add the diced tomato, tomato paste, and oregano and cook until the flavors meld, another 4 to 5 minutes.

Add the chopped basil and gently fold in the spaghetti squash, fully incorporating the sauce into the squash.

Adjust the seasoning with salt and pepper and serve.

ZUCCHINI AL PASTOR

WITH YOGURT

There's a lot to love about Southern California taco culture, but one of my favorites is tacos al pastor. It's a marinated preparation of pork in which the meat is layered with pineapple and grilled on a spit over open flames or coals. The fat from the pork and the juice from the pineapple work magic together on the meat, which is sliced and served in fresh tortillas. My love for that technique inspired this vegetarian dish that is a whimsical collision of al pastor and the flavors of a Mediterranean gyro—two of my favorite meals, to be honest. Truly, I wouldn't be mad if you served this in a pita!

2 pounds uniformly sized large zucchinis

Grapeseed oil, for cooking

Garlic & Mint Yogurt Sauce (page 30), for serving

FOR THE MARINADE

2 cloves garlic, minced

½ cup pineapple juice (see Notes)

1½ teaspoons apple cider vinegar

1 tablespoon achiote paste (see Notes)

1 tablespoon honey or agave nectar

1 tablespoon tomato paste

1 teaspoon ancho chili powder

1 teaspoon ground coriander

1 teaspoon ground cumin

1 teaspoon dried oregano (leaves or ground)

½ teaspoon ground cloves

¼ teaspoon chipotle powder

SPECIAL EQUIPMENT

3 (12-inch) bamboo skewers

Trim the rounded ends off the zucchinis, then slice the zucchinis lengthwise into ¼-inch-thick sheets. Stack the sheets one on top of the other until you have a tall tower of zucchini. Then skewer through the broad side of the zucchini sheets, using three long bamboo skewers spaced about 1 inch apart to hold the stack together. (Think of a club sandwich toothpick method here.) Set aside in a shallow pan, bowl, or food storage container.

In a small bowl, mix together the ingredients for the marinade.

Pour the marinade over the skewered zucchini and, using a pastry brush or your fingers, brush or massage the marinade on all sides. Transfer to the refrigerator and let marinate for a few hours or overnight for the best flavor.

When ready to cook, remove the skewered zucchini from the marinade and preheat a grill or grill pan to medium-high heat.

Brush the grill grates with oil or pour a small amount of oil into the grill pan. Place the skewers on the grill or in the pan and cook, turning often so they cook evenly on all sides, until the zucchini is tender throughout. They will need just a few minutes per side.

Remove the skewers, top with the yogurt sauce, and serve.

NOTES

If you don't have pineapple juice, orange juice would be an acceptable alternative.

Achiote, or annatto, paste is made from seeds that give everything they come into contact with a brilliant reddish orange color. It's what a lot of food brands turn to instead of red food dye. It's natural, and you can sprinkle it on anything you want without imbuing too much flavor. It's great for dyeing fabrics and Easter eggs too!

GLUTEN-FREE PUMPKIN BREAD

OPTION

Do you even know it's fall if you don't make or eat something pumpkin spice flavored? This is an easy one-bowl quick bread that is also gluten free. It goes quickly in our house. Be ready with some good butter to slather on a slice before it's gone.

1 cup pumpkin puree

1 large egg

½ cup granulated monk fruit sweetener (see Notes)

2 tablespoons unsweetened applesauce

2 tablespoons maple syrup

1 tablespoon coconut oil, melted

1 teaspoon vanilla extract

½ cup plain unsweetened almond milk

1 teaspoon ground cinnamon

⅛ teaspoon ginger powder

½ teaspoon salt

3½ teaspoons baking powder

1¼ cups almond meal

1¼ cups all-purpose gluten-free flour

1¼ cups gluten-free old-fashioned oats

FOR SERVING
Butter (optional)

Flaky sea salt

Place a rack in the lower third of the oven and preheat the oven to 350°F (see Notes). Grease the bottom and sides of a 9 by 5-inch loaf pan.

In a large mixing bowl, whisk the pumpkin puree, egg, sweetener, applesauce, maple syrup, coconut oil, vanilla, and almond milk until combined.

Add the spices, salt, and baking powder and whisk again to combine.

Switching to a wooden spoon, fold in the almond meal, flour, and oats just until evenly distributed. The batter will be thick.

Spoon the batter evenly into the prepared loaf pan. Bake for 60 to 75 minutes, until a toothpick inserted in the center comes out clean. If the top is browned before the center is set, loosely tent the pan with foil and continue baking until the loaf is fully baked.

Remove from the oven, set the pan on a wire rack, and let cool in the pan for 20 minutes. When ready to serve, remove the loaf from the pan and slice. Serve each slice with a good dollop of butter and a sprinkle of flaky salt.

NOTES

Monk fruit is a small round fruit native to Asia. It's used to create a no-calorie sweetener that is heat stable and can be used effectively in baked goods. There are monk fruit replacements for granulated sugar, brown sugar, powdered sugar, and liquid sweeteners, and they're easy to find at grocery stores. The type we are using here is often labeled as "classic" or "plant-based sugar alternative" and can be substituted 1:1 in recipes calling for granulated sugar.

If using a glass loaf pan, reduce the oven temperature to 325°F.

To make this recipe dairy free, omit the butter or use a plant-based alternative.

CHOCOLATE SQUASH MOUSSE

When our oldest was in preschool, the school kitchen made an avocado chocolate mousse that the kids just gobbled up. Hidden nutrition was in its nascent days back then. Now, I think we've all grown a bit wiser and know that we don't always have to hide good ingredients; instead, we want to focus on making food delicious. We'll leave it up to you whether you clue your family in to the ingredients of this simple pudding. We like the added fiber, vitamins, and minerals that you get from the squash, and you can be flexible with the sweetener. Honey, date syrup, liquid stevia, and maple syrup all work well.

1 medium acorn squash (about 1 pound), quartered and seeded

2 to 3 ounces dark chocolate (at least 60% cacao), chopped

Liquid sweetener of choice, to taste

1 cup heavy whipping cream, chilled

½ teaspoon vanilla extract

Fill a medium-sized saucepan with water and bring to a boil. Add the quartered squash and simmer until fork-tender, 10 to 12 minutes.

Drain the squash and scoop the flesh into a food processor. Purée until smooth.

Return the puréed squash to the pan and stir in the chopped chocolate until melted and uniform; if needed, set the pan over low heat to warm the mixture slightly and encourage the chocolate to fully melt. Stir in sweetener to taste.

Transfer the puree to a bowl to cool for an hour. Once cool, you can place it in an airtight container and store it in the refrigerator for up to 3 days.

In a large mixing bowl, whisk the cream and vanilla until soft peaks form. (If using an electric mixer, whisk on medium speed, being careful not to overbeat.) Refrigerate until ready to use.

Using a rubber spatula, gently fold the whipped cream into the squash puree. Distribute the mousse evenly among four 5-ounce coupe glasses or small serving bowls and refrigerate for another hour before serving.

CARROTS

The other day, which actually was probably one year ago or so as you're reading this, I thought to myself that the only thing I cook perfectly is glazed carrots—a simple dish of chopped carrots cooked in water and maybe a sprig of lavender and a squeeze of honey and pat of butter. I make this dish frequently for my family, and it never gets a complaint, shrug, sigh, or ugh. Parents get this! Chef parents might get it even more! You can labor over a multi-course meal and the only thing the kids compliment is the carrots. C'est la vie!

Of course, carrots are visually stunning—big, bright, and orange or purple or yellow or even white. They're a veritable rainbow! But I love carrots for being sweet. As you cook along in this book, you'll notice that there isn't a lot of added sugar in the recipes. Finding plant-based recipes that are naturally sweet and being able to taste and register them as sweet (which will happen as you wean yourself away from added sugar) is paramount. It does take some time to reset your palate; in my experience, three to four weeks of removing added sugar usually does the trick.

Speaking of sugar, carrots can be cake! Which always blows my molecular chef mind when I think about someone somewhere, hundreds of years ago, shredding them into a cake in a pinch. In pre–Industrial Revolution times, sugar was hard to come by and expensive, so people turned to natural sweetness to imbue their cooking with that playful dance of sugar. So, yes, using shredded carrots or beets in cake has worked for ages, and now we can turn to this same trick for the health angle as well.

And whether it's your doctor's or your optometrist's endorsement, carrots have long enjoyed marquee status as a good-for-you vegetable. How many times have you heard the adage that carrots are good for your eyesight? It's true (we'll get to that in a minute), but carrots are no one-trick vegetable. They contain significant amounts of magnesium, iron, potassium, and calcium. They also have high amounts of fiber, nature's scrub brush that helps fight water retention and aids in regularity. Even more distinguishing, carrots are a functional food—a food that has benefits beyond its nutritional value. Carrots have been studied extensively for their antioxidant properties, their cancer-fighting abilities, and their effect on heart health, and, yes, they actually are good for your eyes. Turns out lots of varietals of carrots (predominantly the yellow- and orange-colored ones) contain lutein and zeaxanthin, which work to improve eye health and prevent macular degeneration. Bugs Bunny was right! Carrots are really good for you, and though we say that about every vegetable in this book, carrots might be the best. Along with their nutritional content, carrots are the most widely cultivated root crop, making them a "you can count on me" vegetable that is easily sourced, keeps well, and has endless uses in the kitchen.

Indeed, carrots are more than just juice, a glazed side, or an avant-garde dessert ingredient. They can be the center of the plate, braised like meat, or charred and grilled, an application usually reserved for softer vegetables like peppers and squash. We always have carrots on our table for big get-togethers and holidays. Maybe as important for the busy home cook, they are also easy to work with and fast to cook. So, what's up, Doc? Time to get more carrots cooking in your kitchen.

CRUNCHY CARROT SLAW

WITH KALE, ALMONDS, APPLES & RAISINS

POV: Your grandma shows up with this relic from the fifties and it blows your mind. But since it's the twenty-first century, we added kale, of course. This salad is a celebration of textural contrast, and it works great as a side, especially for a charred steak, or as a topping for grilled fish. We love a good remix on a classic dish, and this one will for sure become a new staple.

1 teaspoon prepared horseradish

Grated zest and juice of 2 lemons

1 teaspoon honey

½ teaspoon chili powder

2 pounds carrots, peeled and shredded

1 bunch Tuscan kale, ribs removed, sliced into ribbons (see Note)

½ small red onion, thinly sliced

2 Granny Smith apples

1½ cups golden raisins, roughly chopped

½ cup sliced almonds

Salt and pepper

Make the dressing: In a large mixing bowl, whisk together the horseradish, lemon zest, half of the lemon juice, the honey, and chili powder until emulsified.

Add the carrots, kale, and onion to the bowl and fold to coat in the dressing.

In a small mixing bowl, mix 2 cups of water with the remaining lemon juice. Grate the apples and soak in the lemon water for a minute to prevent oxidation. Drain the apples and add them to the carrot mixture.

Fold in the raisins and almonds until evenly incorporated. Season with salt and pepper to taste.

Serve immediately or chill for a few hours before serving.

NOTE
We prefer the Tuscan variety of kale because it's a bit softer than traditional green kale. The carrots provide a great texture here, and the Tuscan kale gives the dish a softer complement.

CARROT COCONUT SOUP
WITH CILANTRO & LEMONGRASS

OPTION

Here's a soup that Jazmin turns to regularly for an easy midweek meal. As with most things that she cooks, the kids love it much more than anything I make. The bonus here is that I love it too. The creaminess of the carrot puree mixed with coconut milk makes this a "cream of" type of soup that you can slurp without guilt. Carrots are bursting with vitamins and minerals, and the fat from the coconut cream gives this dish some serious satiating power. I like mine with the spicy addition of Thai red curry paste, which plays excellently with coconut and sweet carrots, but the kids prefer it without.

4 tablespoons ghee

2 pounds carrots, peeled and sliced into coins (about 4 cups)

1 medium yellow onion, chopped

3 cloves garlic, sliced

1 teaspoon salt

2 cups chicken or vegetable stock

1 cup no-added-sugar carrot juice or water

1 (13.5-ounce) can coconut milk

2 teaspoons coconut aminos

2 teaspoons Thai red curry paste (optional)

1 stalk lemongrass, root end trimmed

1 tablespoon peeled and grated fresh ginger

1 bay leaf

FOR GARNISH

½ cup chopped fresh cilantro

½ cup salted roasted peanuts, chopped (optional)

Heat a large soup pot with a well-fitting lid over medium-high heat. Melt the ghee in the pot, then add the carrots, onion, and garlic. Season with the salt. Allow to cook undisturbed for a few minutes, until the carrots have some color, then stir and repeat for another 5 to 7 minutes. You don't want a dark char here, just nice toasty brown color and a caramelization of the natural sugars in the carrots. Reduce the heat if the carrots are getting too much color too quickly.

Add the stock, carrot juice, coconut cream, coconut aminos, and curry paste, if using, and bring to a simmer.

Place the lemongrass stalk on a cutting board and, using the back of a knife, gently tap the stalk to release its aromatics. Add the stalk to the pot. Then add the ginger and bay leaf and swirl to incorporate.

Place the lid on the pot, reduce the heat to medium-low, and cook at a gentle simmer for 25 minutes. Remove and discard the lemongrass stalk and bay leaf. Transfer the soup to a blender (work in batches if necessary to avoid overfilling the blender) and purée until smooth.

Serve in bowls and top with the cilantro and, if desired, roasted peanuts.

NOTE
To make this recipe vegetarian, use vegetable stock rather than chicken stock.

GRILLED CARROTS

OPTION   OPTION

Grilled carrots are a clutch recipe for me and most of my restaurants, and here we're giving you two options for dressing them up. Grilling vegetables is a great way to make use of a hot grill, maximize flavor, and open up a world of new vegetable options. Charring—and, yes, it's OK to say burning—is a concept you need to get behind. Think back to the best Mexican salsa you've ever had, and we'll bet something in that salsa was charred or burnt. The grill gives foods a depth of flavor and richness, and in this case, carrots go through a metamorphosis that brings out their natural sweetness, creating an almost carrot caramel on the palate.

2 tablespoons plus 2 teaspoons salt, divided

2 pounds carrots, peeled and cut in half lengthwise if large

Cooking oil, for the grill

1 tablespoon olive oil

2 teaspoons freshly ground black pepper

Grilled Jalapeño Chimichurri or Horseradish Ranch (recipes follow), for serving

Fill a large mixing bowl with ice and water to create an ice bath.

Preheat a grill to medium-high heat.

Fill a large pot with water and add 2 tablespoons of the salt. Bring to a rolling boil and drop in the carrots. Cook until the tip of a knife slides through the thickest part with light resistance, 6 to 8 minutes.

Drain the carrots and plunge them into the ice bath to cool. Remove from the ice water and pat dry.

Brush the grates of the grill lightly with cooking oil.

Place the carrots in a large mixing bowl and toss with the olive oil, the remaining 2 teaspoons of salt, and the pepper.

Line the carrots in a single layer on the grill. Grill on all sides, turning as needed, until well charred. This should take 4 to 5 minutes. Remove and serve with the sauce of your choice.

...WITH GRILLED JALAPEÑO CHIMICHURRI

For this take, we're contrasting the sweetness of the carrots with the herbaceous kick of the jalapeño, which is grilled alongside the carrots. Might as well grill a ribeye steak to go with it, if you're into that kind of thing.

(Makes 1 scant cup)

1 jalapeño pepper

2 cups fresh parsley sprigs

½ cup fresh tarragon leaves

¼ cup fresh basil sprigs

¼ cup fresh mint leaves

Juice of 1 lemon

2 teaspoons capers, drained

1 teaspoon anchovy paste

Up to ½ cup olive oil

2 cloves garlic, peeled

¼ medium white onion, chopped

½ teaspoon salt

½ teaspoon freshly ground black pepper

While you're grilling the carrots, also grill the jalapeño, turning until it is charred on all sides, about 5 minutes.

Chop the grilled jalapeño and place in a food processor along with the herbs, lemon juice, capers, anchovy paste, ¼ cup of olive oil, the garlic cloves, onion, salt, and pepper. Pulse until the mixture has a chunky salsa-like texture. Add more olive oil if needed to process. You can decide how chunky or smooth you'd like it to be.

Transfer the grilled carrots to a large mixing bowl and toss with the chimichurri, or simply spoon the chimichurri over the carrots. Serve warm.

... WITH HORSERADISH RANCH

Carrots and ranch are a slam dunk—they go together like peanut butter and jelly. We're elevating the vibe a bit here by adding some horseradish to the mix. Enjoy!

(Makes 1¼ cups)

2 tablespoons bacon drippings (optional but highly recommended for flavor)

½ cup plain kefir

½ cup avocado oil mayonnaise

2 teaspoons coconut aminos

2 teaspoons red wine vinegar or sherry vinegar

1½ teaspoons prepared horseradish

1 teaspoon dried dill weed

½ teaspoon dried chives

½ teaspoon dried parsley

½ teaspoon garlic powder

½ teaspoon onion powder

Juice of ½ lemon

Pinch of salt

Grind or two of black pepper

Warm the bacon drippings, if using, until they are liquidy and not solid.

Place all of the ingredients in a blender and blend, or shake vigorously in a mason jar with a lid. The dressing should have a paintlike consistency. Depending on the thickness of the kefir you use, you may need to add more kefir if the dressing is too thick or more mayo if it's too thin.

Place the grilled carrots in a large mixing bowl and toss with ½ cup of the ranch dressing, or serve the ranch on the side as a dip. Store leftover ranch in an airtight container in the refrigerator for up to 5 days.

NOTE

To make this recipe dairy free, serve the carrots with chimichurri. To make it vegetarian, serve the carrots with horseradish ranch, omitting the bacon drippings.

CHICKEN SHAWARMA & SPICY CARROT HUMMUS

SERVES 4

WITH GRILLED ZA'ATAR NAAN

OPTION

Is this technically a hummus? If you have wings instead of arms, are you an airplane? Maybe? But let's make peace with the concept that any vegetable or legume can be cooked and puréed and transformed into a delicious and luxurious spread. You could even omit the chickpeas here and double down on the carrots. Tahini is the key, and lately I've been treating it like miso, adding it to dishes for depth and maturity.

FOR THE MARINADE AND CHICKEN

Juice of 1 lemon

2 tablespoons olive oil

6 cloves garlic, minced

1 teaspoon salt

2 teaspoons freshly ground black pepper

2 teaspoons ground cumin

2 teaspoons paprika

½ teaspoon turmeric powder

2 pounds boneless, skinless chicken thighs

FOR THE HUMMUS

Salt

1 lemon

1 pound carrots, peeled and roughly chopped (about 2 cups)

1 (15-ounce) can chickpeas, drained and rinsed

½ cup tahini

½ cup peeled roasted garlic cloves, or 1 teaspoon garlic powder

2 teaspoons ground cumin

2 teaspoons chopped Calabrian chili peppers (packed in oil)

Salt and pepper

FOR THE NAAN

Olive oil

4 plain naan breads

1½ teaspoons za'atar spice

FOR GARNISH

1 bunch fresh cilantro, chopped

Grated lemon zest (from above)

1 cup crumbled feta cheese or plant-based feta

1 teaspoon flaky sea salt

BARBECUED CARROTS

WITH TOMATO, CORIANDER & HONEY

This recipe exists as a close cousin to the Grilled Carrots with Grilled Jalapeño Chimichurri recipe on page 178. They differ in that here, the carrots are cooked entirely in a pan, creating more of a caramelized and roasted texture than a char-grilled one. Not to mention, instead of full-sized carrots, we're using a lunchbox favorite in this recipe: baby carrots. With their small surface area, you'll find that, once cooked in the sauce, these carrots take on a fruit roll-up type of vibe. If you are of a certain age, you'll understand this reference fully.

1 pound baby carrots

1 teaspoon salt

1 teaspoon freshly ground black pepper

2½ tablespoons olive oil, divided

1 shallot, finely diced

1½ teaspoons ghee

1 tablespoon tomato paste

2 tablespoons honey

1 teaspoon coriander seeds, toasted and cracked or ground

½ cup fresh cilantro leaves

In a medium-sized mixing bowl, toss the carrots with the salt, pepper, and 2 tablespoons of the olive oil.

Heat a large heavy-bottomed skillet over medium-high heat. Transfer the seasoned carrots and oil to the pan and sear on all sides, 10 to 12 minutes total. Remove the carrots from the pan and set aside.

Using the same skillet, cook the shallot in the ghee over medium heat for about a minute while stirring. Stir in the tomato paste and cook for another 2 to 3 minutes, until fragrant.

Whisk in the honey, coriander, and remaining ½ tablespoon of olive oil. Return the carrots to the skillet and toss with the sauce until completely coated and fork-tender.

Remove from the heat and stir in the cilantro. Serve warm.

LAMB BRAISED CARROTS
WITH DUKKAH & YOGURT

OPTION

One way to get a meaty flavor without the actual meat is to use their essence—which sounds so much better than fat, doesn't it? But fat is flavor, and lamb flavor is a perfect match for dukkah spice and yogurt. We use a lot of fat here, but don't be afraid; it's necessary for the "confit" cooking process. You will be cooking the carrots in the fat and removing them to eat. Lamb tallow, or fat, can be hard to source, so you can certainly use bacon drippings or olive oil instead, and it will still be delicious. This book is about elevating your plant and vegetable game, though, so if you want to go next-level, talk to your local butcher about lamb tallow and follow this road map!

1 tablespoon ghee

2 pounds carrots, peeled and cut into large pieces

1 teaspoon salt

½ teaspoon freshly ground black pepper

1½ to 2 cups melted rendered lamb fat (aka lamb tallow), bacon drippings, or olive oil (see Notes)

2 cloves garlic, smashed with the side of a knife

4 to 5 sprigs fresh thyme

2 bay leaves

1 teaspoon black peppercorns

FOR GARNISH

1 cup plain Greek yogurt

1 tablespoon dukkah spice blend (see Note)

1 tablespoon chopped fresh dill

1 tablespoon chopped fresh mint

Grated zest and juice of 1 lemon

Heat a large, deep heavy-bottomed skillet with a well-fitting lid over medium heat. Melt the ghee in the pan. Add the carrots, season with the salt and pepper, and char on all sides.

Pour the lamb fat over the carrots; they should be at least halfway covered in the fat. Add the garlic, thyme, bay leaves, and peppercorns. Lower the heat and bring to a gentle simmer. Cover and continue cooking until the carrots are fork-tender, about 35 minutes. Remove the pan from the heat.

Remove the carrots from the fat and place on paper towels. If desired, reserve the fat for further use.

To serve, spoon ¼ cup of the yogurt onto the bottom of each bowl. Top with the cooked carrots and finish with the dukkah spice, dill, mint, and lemon zest and juice.

NOTES

Dukkah is a blend of herbs, nuts, and spices. I've seen it at Trader Joe's, so I think it's tipping into popularity. You can also seek it out from an online vendor.

If using bacon fat, use ½ teaspoon salt instead of the full teaspoon.

To make this recipe vegetarian (if a bit less delicious), cook the carrots in olive oil rather than lamb fat or bacon drippings.

CHARRED CARROT HOT DOGS

OPTION

Sometimes an idea is silly and obvious. Sometimes silly and obvious can also be delicious. There's no magic here except that a peeled carrot looks like a hot dog and tastes like one after it's spiced with the right seasonings that make a hot dog more than just emulsified meat. Cook it in beef drippings instead of olive oil and you may get the same ballpark vibes you get from the real thing—without the burps! Actually, that's unverified, but it is less meat, more flavor, better health.

Salt

12 medium carrots (about hot dog diameter and 8 inches long), peeled and ends trimmed

FOR THE HOT DOG SPICE MIX

2 tablespoons olive oil

1 tablespoon paprika

1 tablespoon dry mustard

1 teaspoon granulated onion

1 teaspoon ground celery seeds

1 teaspoon salt

1 teaspoon freshly ground black pepper

½ teaspoon ground coriander

½ teaspoon ground mace

¼ teaspoon freshly grated nutmeg

12 hot dog buns

3 tablespoons ghee, melted

2 cups sauerkraut

Deli mustard, for serving

Preheat a grill or grill pan to medium-high heat.

Bring a large pot of salted water to a boil. Add the carrots and simmer for 8 minutes, or until the tip of a knife slides in with some resistance. Drain the carrots and set aside.

In a large mixing bowl, whisk together the hot dog spice mix ingredients. Add the carrots and toss to coat evenly in the seasoning mixture.

Grill the carrots until well charred on all sides, about a minute per side. Lightly brush the hot dog buns with the ghee and toast on the grill until warmed and slightly crispy on the edges.

To serve, place the carrots in the buns and top with the sauerkraut and some mustard.

NOTE
To make this recipe gluten free, use gluten-free buns.

CARROT OSSO BUCO

WITH POLENTA

OPTION

The year was 1999, and I was a fresh-faced boy straight from the Culinary Institute of America learning under some of the world's best chefs in their Michelin-starred restaurants. As was often the case with new team members, I was left to monitor, skim, strain, and store the huge vats of stock used in classic French kitchens. The dredge of those pots was filled with meaty bones cooked to remove their last drop of flavor and the accompanying mirepoix of onions, celery, and carrots. The vegetables left in the strainer were a revelation to me. Chock-full of flavor, umami, and salinity, but often discarded, they carry all the gravitas of the main protein they simmered with. These luscious spoonfuls of vegetables that I'd sneak as lunch created a flavor memory for me that I now share with you. Here we are treating the carrots as we would the veal in a traditional osso buco recipe by braising them in stock and wine. The porcini powder adds the bite of umami that is sometimes missing in vegetarian dishes.

Salt

8 ounces pearl onions

1 tablespoon plus 1 teaspoon olive or avocado oil

6 horse carrots, scrubbed and cut crosswise into 3 or 4 chunks each (see Notes)

Freshly ground black pepper

2 teaspoons curry powder

2 cups dry red wine

1 tablespoon porcini mushroom powder (see Notes)

2 cups vegetable or chicken stock

2 teaspoons coconut aminos

2 teaspoons red wine vinegar

½ cup fresh flat-leaf parsley (mostly leaves), chopped, for garnish

FOR THE POLENTA

2 quarts plain unsweetened cashew milk or other nondairy milk alternative of choice

1 bay leaf

½ teaspoon ground cloves

2 teaspoons salt

½ teaspoon freshly ground black pepper

2 cups yellow polenta or finely ground cornmeal

Preheat the oven to 350°F.

Fill a small pot halfway with water, season with a couple pinches of salt, and bring to a rolling boil. Cook the onions in the boiling water for 1 minute. Drain the onions and let cool to the touch, then trim their ends and peel them.

Heat 1 tablespoon of the oil in a heavy-bottomed roasting pan (or a Dutch oven) over medium-high heat. Add the carrots in a single layer and season with 2 teaspoons of salt and 1 teaspoon of pepper. Lower the heat to medium and cook, turning the carrots frequently, until browned on all sides, 8 to 10 minutes.

Fold the onions and curry powder into the carrots and cook for another minute.

Pour in the wine and bring to a simmer. Cook for 3 minutes, or until the wine has reduced by about half.

Add the porcini powder, stock, and coconut aminos and bring to a boil.

Transfer the pan to the oven, uncovered, and braise the carrots for about 1 hour, until fork-tender. Stir the contents of the pan about halfway through the cooking time.

Meanwhile, make the polenta: Put the cashew milk, bay leaf, cloves, salt, and pepper in a large saucepan and bring to a boil over medium-high heat.

Once boiling, whisk in the polenta. Continue whisking until it returns to a low simmer, reduce the heat to medium, and cook, whisking frequently to prevent sticking, until the mixture is very thick, about 30 minutes. Remove and discard the bay leaf.

Once the carrots are fork-tender, remove them from the oven and finish the braising sauce in the pan by adding the vinegar and seasoning with salt and pepper to taste. Stir gently to incorporate the ingredients, taking care not to break or mash the carrots.

To serve, spoon the polenta into serving bowls, top with the carrots and onions, and then drizzle copiously with the sauce. Garnish with the chopped parsley.

NOTES

"Horse" carrots aren't always labeled as such; what you're looking for are real chunky, thick carrots. Think 3 inches in diameter at least.

Porcini powder can be found in a fair number of produce sections nowadays. If not, online specialty stores carry it, as does Amazon.

To make this recipe vegetarian, use vegetable stock rather than chicken stock.

GLUTEN-FREE CARROT CAKE

OPTION

We recently made this recipe for Mother's Day and debated the merits of carrot cake. Is it really cake, or is it quick bread? Does it taste of carrots? Is it for people who wouldn't normally eat carrots? We covered all this as we devoured this healthier-than-normal dessert. We made it into a layer cake, but we presume you could cook it as a loaf and double the cook time. Then you'd have carrot bread, and that is markedly less exciting than carrot CAKE! Either way, get ready for a delicious treat with a vegetable star.

2 packed cups blanched superfine almond flour

½ cup coconut flour, spooned and leveled

1 teaspoon baking soda

1 teaspoon ground cinnamon

¼ teaspoon ground nutmeg

⅛ teaspoon ground cloves

⅛ teaspoon ginger powder

½ teaspoon salt

4 large eggs, room temperature

¾ cup maple syrup

⅓ cup unsalted cashew butter, room temperature (see Notes)

¼ cup plain unsweetened almond, coconut, or cashew milk

1½ teaspoons vanilla extract

⅓ cup coconut oil, melted and cooled

3 cups peeled and shredded carrots

½ cup chopped Sprouted Walnuts (page 48), plus more for garnish if desired

½ cup raisins (optional)

Unsweetened shredded coconut, for garnish (optional)

FOR THE CREAM CHEESE FROSTING

½ cup (1 stick) unsalted butter, room temperature (see Notes)

1 (8-ounce) package vegan cream cheese, room temperature

2½ cups powdered sugar or zero-calorie powdered sugar replacement

2 teaspoons vanilla extract

1 to 2 tablespoons plain unsweetened almond, coconut, or cashew milk

Preheat the oven to 350°F. Line the bottoms of two 8-inch round cake pans with parchment paper. Spray the parchment and the sides of each pan with ghee cooking spray.

In a medium-sized mixing bowl, whisk together the flours, baking soda, spices, and salt.

In a large mixing bowl, whisk together the eggs, maple syrup, cashew butter, milk, and vanilla until smooth.

Pour the cooled liquid coconut oil into the wet ingredients and whisk well. Fold in the carrots.

Add the dry ingredients one-third at a time to the wet ingredients and mix until well combined. The batter will be thick. Fold in the walnuts and the raisins, if using.

Split the batter evenly between the prepared pans. Use a rubber spatula or wooden spoon to spread it evenly and smooth the tops.

Place the cakes side by side on the middle rack of the oven. Bake for 25 to 30 minutes, until a tester inserted in the center of a cake comes out clean. Set the pans on a wire rack and allow the cakes to cool completely in the pans, about 1 hour.

While the cakes are cooling, make the frosting: In the bowl of a stand mixer or in a large mixing bowl with a hand mixer, beat the room-temperature butter and cream cheese on high speed until light and fluffy. With the mixer running on low speed, slowly add the powdered sugar and vanilla and continue to beat for another minute. Add 1 tablespoon of the milk and beat for another minute or two, adding up to another tablespoon of milk if needed to achieve an acceptable frosting consistency. Set the frosting aside.

Once the cakes have cooled completely, remove one layer from the pan by placing one hand on top of the cake and gently flipping the pan over a plate. If there is any resistance, slide a knife between the edge of the pan and the cake and then try flipping again. Gently slide your hand out from under the cake to lay it on the plate, top side down. Spread about one-third of the frosting on the top of the cake. Repeat with the second cake layer, placing it on the first layer top side up, then frost the top and sides of the cake with the remaining frosting.

You can decorate the cake with chopped walnuts and shredded coconut if you like. Store the cake in the refrigerator until ready to eat. It should keep well for up to 5 days, but ours disappears in one day.

NOTES

For the cashew butter, a spreadable loose consistency is perfect. If your cashew butter is too thick (or just puréed cashews), you can stir in up to 1 tablespoon of melted coconut oil.

The frosting is kept for the most part dairy free with the exception of the butter, which adds a negligible amount of dairy even for dairy-intolerant people. If it's an issue for you, you can replace it with the plant-based butter of your choice.

MUSHROOMS

I'm a pretty fun guy (fun-gi) when it comes to mushrooms. I know they can be polarizing, but they come in a variety of types, textures, and even flavors, and they really do bring an earthiness, even a meatiness, to any meal.

Most everyone is familiar with the grocery store staple, the white button mushroom. It's mild-tasting, a bit toothsome, and widely available year-round. This type has grown wild since prehistoric times. In France, it was first cultivated underground in catacombs. Even the plain button mushroom has some true provenance! However, there are hundreds (maybe thousands) of other varietals of edible mushrooms, along with many poisonous and noxious varietals. So, even though the next few paragraphs aim to inspire you to try mushrooms far and wide, make sure you procure them from grocery stores, farmers' markets, and/or credible foragers.

Mushrooms can be great training wheels for people who are trying to become vegetarian or vegan or who are just replacing a few meals a week with plant-based options. They fill the hole that removing meat from a dish can leave for some people. Maybe that's because they're physiologically closer to animals than plants. It's true! Plants are considered autotrophs because they create their own food. Humans and mushrooms are heterotrophs, meaning they depend on outside sources for glucose and other nutrients.

Mushrooms and meat share another surprising attribute: both provide the elusive fifth primary taste, umami. *Umami* is a Japanese word that translates to "essence of deliciousness." It is a long-lasting, complex, mouthwatering taste. Simply defined, it is the taste of something savory. Umami can be found in crave-worthy meals like bacon cheeseburgers, fettuccine Alfredo, and pepperoni pizza. But if you eat those meals every day, you'll be feeling pretty crummy. Luckily, umami is prevalent not just in meat and mushrooms, but also in tomatoes, onions, and other produce. It is why many mushrooms can swap in so easily for meat and why, for most recipes, I much prefer using minced mushrooms rather than a plant-based meat replacement. They have a great texture that holds up well even to braising or longer cooking times. Besides all of these pluses, mushrooms are rife with vitamin D, potassium, selenium, zinc, and folate. They are simply magical ingredients.

Luckily, I like all mushrooms, and so does my family (well, most of them). For the recipes in this chapter, we encourage you to expand beyond the button mushroom and try other types. Portobellos, morels, shiitakes, and even enoki mushrooms are easy to find in most supermarkets and will give you a great breadth of flavor and texture. I particularly like porcinis. They are on the expensive side because many are wild harvested seasonally, and growing them commercially has proved difficult and costly. The end result, though, is a dreamy-textured white mushroom with umami to spare. Morels are Jazmin's favorite. They're complex, earthy, and elegant, just like her. You can sauté them in a knob of butter with salt and pepper in the springtime for an easy, perfect dish.

If there's anything that has marked the mushroom world of the 2020s, it's the emergence and availability of adaptogens. Adaptogens are not a new comic superhero team but a category of active ingredients found in plants that help you deal with stress, fatigue, and anxiety by targeting specific stress receptors in the body. And a lot of adaptogens are mushrooms! Maybe while scrolling through Instagram or perusing your natural food store, you've seen the words *reishi, lion's mane,* and *cordyceps*. These are all examples of adaptogens that you can add to food or beverages. We didn't include adaptogens specifically in these recipes, but we've been known to add some to smoothies (see pages 150 to 153) and baked goods (such as cookies, page 276, and pumpkin bread, page 166). *Note:* Always check with your doctor before adding adaptogens to your diet because they can interfere with certain medications.

I've always said that if things ever go sideways on me, I will march into the woods to find mushrooms to cook and eat under the stars and conifers. I had this escape plan well before watching Nicolas Cage's reclusive character in the movie *Pig* (which, by the way, is great—a must-watch). I don't know what chef consulted on that film, but maybe the run-away-to-the-forest plan is a common coping mechanism for restaurant chefs!

And finally, speaking of pigs, you'll notice that we use truffle oil a good bit in this chapter. Although most truffle oil is chemically produced, some is derived from the wild truffle, which was traditionally foraged using specially trained truffle pigs. (And pigs make bacon, and we arrive at Kevin Bacon in only three steps. Voilà!) Truffles and mushrooms go together famously, but truffles are not mushrooms as many people think. Although truffles are in the fungus kingdom, they are actually tubers, like yams and Jerusalem artichokes. Where mushrooms and truffles collide is in their earthy woodsiness and their ability to elevate the depth of a dish. Great restaurants often use them in tandem, and the combination adds an air of sophistication to a home-cooked meal.

PORCINI OMU-LETTE

OK, friend (we are friends now, right?), you are about to make one of the most challenging recipes in this book, and your enthusiasm is needed! This is the famous Japanese omurice dish, where eggs ooze over a bed of rice. Traditionally, it's served with a drizzle of ketchup, but we are cutting out sugar and processed foods, so we're using a savory, umami-rich, vegetarian demi-glace instead. It is a rich and textural experience. And I'm not just talking about the final product. It took me a few tries to get even close to the classic presentation. You want a runny omelette that blossoms open when cut, but truth be told, the first few times you'll probably end up making a beautiful omelette instead of an omu-lette. If you're determined to get the knack of the traditional omurice technique, I suggest you check out a few YouTube or Instagram videos to see the full expression of the dish.

1 tablespoon heavy cream or melted and cooled unsalted butter

3 large eggs

2 tablespoons Vegetarian Demi-Glace (page 52)

1 cup Cauliflower Fried Rice (page 82)

1 cup fresh porcini mushrooms, cleaned and sliced (see Note)

1 tablespoon unsalted butter

Pinch of salt

Pinch of freshly ground black pepper

2 teaspoons sliced fresh chives, for garnish

Thoroughly whisk the cream or cooled melted butter with the eggs.

Warm the demi-glace and leftover fried rice.

In a sauté pan over medium heat, cook the mushrooms in the butter until golden. Season with the salt and pepper and set aside.

Grease a 12-inch nonstick skillet with ghee or avocado oil cooking spray and heat over high heat. Add the whisked eggs, lay the mushrooms on top, and immediately turn off the heat while folding the eggs into a crescent shape in the pan. This whole process will take 60 to 90 seconds max. The eggs will still be runny.

Lay the fried rice in the center of a plate, mimicking the shape and length of your omelette. Position the fragile omelette atop the rice, seam side down.

Slice the runny omelette lengthwise down the center with a sharp knife, allowing it to open and drape over the edges of the rice. Pour the warm demi-glace over the top. Garnish with the chives.

NOTE

Fresh porcinis can be difficult to find because they're always gathered in the wild, never cultivated. They are more likely to be sold at a farmers' market than a grocery store. Look for them in late summer and autumn, when they are in season. If you can't find fresh porcinis, substitute fresh creminis plus 1 tablespoon porcini mushroom powder, which is stocked in a fair number of produce sections nowadays. If not, online specialty stores carry it, as does Amazon.

SHAVED BUTTON MUSHROOM SALAD
WITH TRUFFLE OIL & LEMON

OPTION OPTION

Confession time: I like canned sliced mushrooms—you know, the kind you get on a mediocre pizza. Well, these are the same mushrooms, but fresh. Here, you take your standard white button mushroom, shave it thin, and simply dress it on the plate like you would a carpaccio. You can add a smattering of soft goat cheese if you'd like, but some chopped parsley is really all it needs.

1½ cups white button mushrooms, stems trimmed

¼ teaspoon salt

¼ teaspoon freshly ground black pepper

1 tablespoon extra-virgin olive oil

2 teaspoons white truffle oil

Juice of ½ lemon

2 tablespoons chopped fresh parsley

3 tablespoons fresh (soft) goat cheese (optional)

Rinse the mushrooms briefly under cold water. Pat dry with a towel, then slice as thin as a quarter (a mandoline can help here, but watch your fingers).

Layer all of the slices as a mosaic on a flat plate and sprinkle with the salt and pepper.

Whisk together the olive oil, truffle oil, and lemon juice and drizzle the mixture over the mushrooms. Garnish with the chopped parsley and, if desired, dollops of goat cheese.

NOTE
To make this recipe dairy free and vegan, omit the goat cheese.

CAULIFLOWER CREPES

WITH MUSHROOMS & PROSCIUTTO

I've made it pretty clear that I'm a savory breakfast guy. Even with Nutella as a solid option, I'm most likely going savory for breakfast and brunch. This is a variation of a classic crepe filled with ham, cheese, and mushrooms. We're relying on our favorite vegan cheese and store-bought gluten-free egg-and-cauliflower wraps here, not just because they provide healthy swaps (they do) but because we truly enjoy the taste! Maybe you will too, and if not, feel free to use the originals. That's one of the biggest takeaways in this book: explore your options in the kitchen and grocery store to expand your eating. Be curious! Just be careful not to pick up something too processed in the process.

1 tablespoon unsalted butter

2 cups cleaned and sliced mushrooms (any type; portobello caps are a great option)

¼ cup diced prosciutto, pancetta, or ham (preferably no added sugar)

½ teaspoon white truffle oil

2 slices vegan provolone or Swiss cheese

2 egg-and-cauliflower wraps/ crepes (see Note)

1 lemon wedge

1 tablespoon sliced fresh chives

In a sauté pan over medium heat, melt the butter until it bubbles.

Add the mushrooms and prosciutto and cook in the frothy butter for 3 to 4 minutes, until the mushrooms start to soften. Stir in the truffle oil. Place the cheese slices on top of the mixture and remove the pan from the heat.

Warm the wraps per the package instructions, then layer half of the mushroom mixture in the center of each wrap. Squeeze the lemon juice over the top and sprinkle on the chives. Fold the crepes in half and serve.

NOTE
We like Crepini's egg-and-cauliflower wraps because they have a similar texture to traditional crepes, and they taste pretty great too.

MUSHROOM TOAST
WITH SHERRY & GOAT CHEESE

This is one of the simplest savory dishes that somehow manages to be a perfect breakfast, snack, or first course for a dinner party. Although we are minding the amount of flour and dairy we are using in this book, we're going with traditional sourdough and fresh goat cheese here. Why? Well, you can swap the sourdough for gluten-free bread and replace the cheese with Cashew Cheese Spread (page 46), Baba Ghanoush (page 230), Spicy Carrot Hummus (page 182), or plain hummus, but I'm not in the business of eliminating ingredients altogether ad infinitum. Indeed, moderation is key, and I'd rather eat some good bread and tart cheese than a greasy fast-food cheeseburger...well, that's true on most days. I'm a work in progress, and so are you!

2 teaspoons olive oil

16 ounces small cremini mushrooms, cleaned and halved if larger than bite-sized

1 tablespoon finely diced yellow onions

1 clove garlic, smashed with the side of a knife

2 sprigs fresh thyme

2 tablespoons dry sherry or white wine

1 tablespoon unsalted butter

Salt and pepper

4 slices sourdough bread

3 tablespoons fresh (soft) goat cheese

1 tablespoon sliced fresh chives

Heat the olive oil in a sauté pan over medium heat. Add the mushrooms, onions, garlic, and thyme sprigs and sauté, tossing occasionally, until the mushrooms are almost cooked and lightly browned, 2 to 3 minutes.

Pull the pan off the heat and pour in the sherry. Being mindful of a possible flambé situation, place the pan back on the burner and cook until most of the liquid has evaporated.

Remove the pan from the heat again, swirl in the butter, and season with salt and pepper to taste. Remove and discard the thyme sprigs.

Toast the bread until it's golden brown, then spread the goat cheese on the bread. Top with the mushroom mixture and sprinkle with the chives.

PORTOBELLO TARTLETTES
WITH BAKED GOAT CHEESE & CARAMELIZED ONIONS

OPTION

To be fair, I'm one of those people who could substitute a portobello cap for just about anything: a hamburger patty, a tart shell, a small bowl, a nice hat...you see where I'm going here. This dish runs along the lines of a nice onion tart with a lot more superfood content. Again, you could substitute cashew cheese or even vegan cream cheese for the goat cheese, and it would still slay.

FOR THE CARAMELIZED ONIONS
(Makes about 1 cup)

2 tablespoons ghee

1 large yellow onion, sliced into half-moons

Salt

Room-temperature water

2 large portobello mushrooms

¼ cup olive oil

2 tablespoons balsamic vinegar

2 tablespoons water

½ cup fresh (soft) goat cheese, Cashew Cheese Spread (page 46), or vegan cream cheese

2 tablespoons sliced fresh chives

White truffle oil (optional)

NOTE
To make this recipe dairy free, use cashew cheese or vegan cream cheese rather than goat cheese.

Preheat the oven to 325°F. Line a sheet pan with aluminum foil.

To make the caramelized onions, melt the ghee in a medium-sized saucepan over medium heat, then add the onion slices and a healthy pinch of salt and reduce the heat to medium-low. Stirring occasionally, slowly cook the onions for about 15 minutes, until blonde-colored and softened. If the pan is dry at this point, add a splash of water, scrape any dried bits off the bottom, and continue to cook the onions for another 15 to 20 minutes, until they turn golden brown. Remove the pan from the heat and set aside.

While the onions are caramelizing, prepare the portobellos: Clean the mushrooms, then remove the stem and scrape the gills from each cap, leaving a beautiful shell. Pour the olive oil, balsamic vinegar, and water into a casserole dish large enough to fit the two mushroom caps and stir to combine. Place the mushroom caps hollow side down in the dish and bake for 25 minutes, basting with the pan juices occasionally.

Transfer the mushrooms to the prepared sheet pan, turning them face up; reserve the juices in the casserole dish.

Fill the mushroom caps with the caramelized onions and top each cap with ¼ cup of the goat cheese. Place the pan in the oven.

After about 15 minutes, when the goat cheese is looking a little melty, turn the oven to broil and broil the tartlettes until lightly browned, hot, and bubbly.

Serve topped with the chives and a drizzle of the reserved mushroom juices. Add a few drops of truffle oil if you have it on hand.

MUSHROOM RISOTTO

OPTION

Risotto: the bane of many cooking show contestants' existence, an overused menu item in the early aughts, the pride of northern Italy. Risotto is many things, but is it healthy and easy? How else could we have gotten it into this book? This is a recipe we've cooked many times at home, and usually while monitoring our dairy intake. We love it because it reduces this rice dish to its essence. If you're really looking for simplicity, you could even forgo the mushrooms here, but we think they're a perfect addition and a nice vehicle to introduce kids to fungi without much heavy lifting. If no kids are present, swap out the button mushrooms for porcinis or morels and serve this by candlelight with some Pinot Noir. And be sure to add the truffle oil; it's optional but pairs so well with the mushrooms and adds a touch of elegance.

2 pints white button mushrooms

½ small white onion

1 clove garlic

1 tablespoon olive oil

2 cups Arborio rice

3 tablespoons unsalted butter

3 tablespoons grated Parmesan cheese, or 1 teaspoon nutritional yeast

Salt and ground white pepper

FOR GARNISH

2 tablespoons sliced fresh chives

¼ cup grated Parmesan cheese (optional)

1½ teaspoons truffle oil (optional)

Bring 1 quart of water to a boil in a small saucepan on one of the back burners of your stovetop and then maintain at a slow simmer.

Clean the mushrooms and trim and discard the stems. Chop the mushrooms into rice-sized pieces by hand or using a food processor. Mince the onion and garlic.

Heat the olive oil in a medium-sized heavy-bottomed pot with a well-fitting lid, preferably earthenware or enamel-coated cast iron, over medium-low heat.

When the oil is glassy, add the onion and cook for a minute or two, until slightly softened. Stir in the garlic and then, a minute later, the mushrooms and cook until everything is fragrant and softened, 2 to 3 minutes more.

Add the rice and cover with enough of the hot water to submerge the rice. Cover the pot and cook until the water has evaporated, about 10 minutes.

Taste the rice for doneness. It should be tender but still have some chew. If it needs a little more cooking, add a few more tablespoons of the hot water, replace the lid, and cook until the water has evaporated. Repeat as necessary until the rice is 95 percent cooked.

Stir in the butter and cheese and remove the pot from the heat. Taste and adjust the seasoning with salt and pepper. The risotto should be just cooked and creamy. When you place it on a plate, it should fall like relaxing shoulders after a sigh.

To serve, top with the chives and, if desired, Parmesan and truffle oil.

NOTE

To make this recipe vegetarian, use nutritional yeast and skip the Parmesan cheese garnish.

THE 50/50 MUSHROOM BURGER

This recipe is beyond delicious. It's a key takeaway too: if you are reducing the amount of animal protein you're consuming, you don't have to take it all away. Cooking *less* meat also makes an impact on your diet and on the environment. That's why meatless Mondays were invented! Being that I'm a chef, this burger recipe maximizes textural gain as well as flavor. The mushrooms provide umami and a nice "fatty" texture that keeps the burger juicy. Not to mention mushrooms are like sponges, so they soak up all of the beef juices and flavor. Is it a little more work? Yes, this is part of the bigger vegetable problem we have. Vegetables demand more labor. Labor of love? Maybe? Labor in the name of health? That's a bit more honest, for me.

3 tablespoons ghee, divided

1 pound mushrooms (any type), cleaned and finely chopped into rice-sized pieces (see Notes)

1 teaspoon granulated garlic

Salt and pepper

1 pound 90/10 grass-fed ground beef

4 slices vegan American cheese (optional)

4 gluten-free hamburger buns

¼ cup Caramelized Onions (see page 212)

¼ cup Quick Pickles (page 38)

Condiments of choice (see Notes)

In a sauté pan over low heat, melt 1 tablespoon of the ghee. Add the chopped mushrooms and granulated garlic, season with a little salt and pepper, and sauté until the mushrooms are soft and have released all of their juices and the liquid has reduced. This could take 15 to 20 minutes, depending on the freshness and type of the mushrooms.

Remove the mushrooms to a bowl and, once no longer warm, place in the refrigerator until chilled; this step can be done earlier in the day or up to a day ahead.

With clean hands, thoroughly mix the chilled mushrooms with the ground beef, then form four patties slightly wider than the buns you are using. Season both sides of the patties with salt and pepper.

Using the same pan, melt 1 tablespoon of the ghee over high heat and sear the burgers until golden brown on both sides, 5 to 7 minutes per side for medium doneness for 1½-inch-thick burgers.

In the last 2 minutes of cooking, top each patty with a slice of cheese, if using, then remove the patties from the pan to rest.

Using the same pan, toast the buns in the remaining tablespoon of ghee. (A nice toast on a hamburger bun is essential!) You can use a paper towel to remove some of the fat from the pan before adding the ghee if you're looking to reduce your caloric intake here.

To assemble the burgers, arrange the onions and pickles on the bottom buns, then top with the burger patties. Garnish the top buns with whatever condiments you'd like and place on the burgers.

NOTES

Any type of mushroom will do here. For convenience and flavor, I use white button mushrooms or shiitakes. Shiitakes give the burgers a bit more of an earthy, smoky flavor, almost mimicking dry-aged beef. Chop the mushrooms by hand or use a food processor.

For condiments, the garlic mayo on page 106 is a simple, flavorful, and non-sugar-laden option. Ketchup and many other store-bought condiments contain lots of added sugar and syrups, so I try to avoid them or make something healthier.

MUSHROOM BOLOGNESE

OPTION OPTION

This recipe builds on what you learned with the 50/50 burger—that mushrooms stand in beautifully both with and for meat in a meat-centric recipe. Here we are using the framework of the iconic pasta dish but omitting the meat altogether. However, if you find yourself rummaging through your fridge (like I often do) and there's a little of this and a little of that, feel free to apply the partly vegetarian ideology and add some ground beef, a knob of salami, some diced pancetta, or whatever you have on hand. But I think the tomato-mushroom sauce is enough of a showstopper that you might be able to tell someone this is a Bolognese without saying it's meatless, and they won't know any different. Leftover wine from the night before is perfect for the sauce.

1 pound gluten-free or whole-wheat rigatoni pasta

1 pound mushrooms (any type), cleaned and stems trimmed

½ cup chopped carrots

1 small yellow onion, chopped

1 tablespoon olive oil

2 cloves garlic, minced

1 teaspoon dried oregano leaves

1 teaspoon fennel seeds

½ teaspoon red pepper flakes, plus more for serving if desired

1 tablespoon tomato paste

1 cup dry white or red wine

1½ cups crushed tomatoes or tomato puree

1 (2- to 4-inch) chunk Parmesan rind

3 tablespoons unsalted butter

2 tablespoons grated Parmesan cheese, plus more for garnish if desired, or ½ teaspoon nutritional yeast

¼ cup chopped fresh parsley

Red pepper flakes, for garnish (optional)

Cook the rigatoni per the package instructions for al dente. Drain and set aside. Do not rinse the pasta.

In a food processor, pulse the mushrooms, carrots, and onion until chopped into rice-sized pieces; the mixture should have the texture of ground meat.

Warm the olive oil in a large heavy-bottomed saucepot over medium heat, then add the mushroom-vegetable mixture and cook, stirring occasionally, until the vegetables have softened a bit and the onion is translucent, about 3 minutes.

Add the garlic, oregano, fennel seeds, and red pepper flakes to the pot and stir to distribute evenly. Mix in the tomato paste and cook for 3 more minutes, or until everything starts to smell amazing.

Deglaze the pot by pouring in the wine and scraping any cooked bits from the bottom of the pot with a wooden spoon, making sure nothing is sticking.

Add the crushed tomatoes and Parmesan rind and cook until the mixture has reduced in volume by at least one-quarter and the flavors start to meld. This will take 20 to 30 minutes.

Fold in the cooked rigatoni to coat it in the sauce. After a quick toss, remove the pot from the heat and fold in the butter, grated Parmesan, and parsley, incorporating them evenly. You don't want to leave it on the heat for too long or your pasta will turn to mush (gluten-free varieties are especially tricky here).

Serve garnished with additional grated Parmesan and/or red pepper flakes, if desired.

NOTE
To make this recipe gluten free, use a gluten-free pasta. To make it vegetarian, omit the Parmesan rind and use nutritional yeast rather than grated Parmesan.

ROAST BEAST

WITH HORSERADISH RANCH & SHERRY-GLAZED MUSHROOMS

SERVES 6 TO 8

Here's a traditional holiday roast—the same one we serve in our house. Maybe you've had your fill of turkey—and for celebrity chefs, this can happen as early as September, as we often are shooting and filming holiday content for media outlets months in advance. A nice standing rib roast is a great alternative to the traditional turkey or ham. It can be as large as you need; every bone will serve one to two people. Some people are scared to cook a large piece of meat, but don't overthink this. Season it aggressively and let it rip in a hot oven! The mushrooms are the star of this dish anyway. They shine because of their simplicity. Add Jazmin's family recipe of mashed rutabaga on page 112, and you'll have a pretty close replica of what we'll be eating this holiday season.

FOR THE ROAST BEAST

1 (6-pound) standing rib roast (aka prime rib)

3 tablespoons Montreal steak seasoning or similar spice blend (no sugar added)

Salt, for finishing

FOR SERVING

1 recipe Horseradish Ranch (page 180)

1 recipe Creamy Mushrooms Glazed in Sherry (page 222)

About an hour before you plan to cook the roast, remove it from the refrigerator and season the meat liberally with the steak seasoning. Allow the roast to come to room temperature.

Preheat the oven to 400°F.

Place the roast fat side up in a roasting pan fitted with a rack and bake for 1 hour.

Lower the heat to 325°F and cook for about 2 hours more. To check for doneness, place a probe thermometer in the deepest center part of the rib and do a temperature check: for rare, it should read 125°F; for medium-rare, 130°F; or for medium, 135°F.

Remove the roast and let it rest for 20 minutes before slicing. The temperature will continue to rise as it rests.

To slice, remove the bones with the first cut and then slice steaks throughout the roast.

Sprinkle some salt on the sliced meat and serve with the horseradish ranch and sherry-glazed mushrooms.

NOTE
If you'd like to cook a smaller or larger roast, use this formula, which will yield medium-rare beef: Cook for 1 hour at 400°F followed by 20 minutes per 1 pound of roast at 325°F.

CREAMY MUSHROOMS

GLAZED IN SHERRY

I serve this as a side dish in a few of my restaurants. It's one of my favorites to add alongside a rib roast or a nice piece of fish, or even atop some risotto. We also make it for every family holiday. You could omit the coconut milk and revel in the simplicity of the earthy mushrooms, but the texture and mouthfeel of "creamy" is, for me, one of the best parts of holiday cooking.

2 pounds small white button or cremini mushrooms

2 tablespoon olive oil

2 sprigs fresh thyme

Salt and pepper

¾ cup dry sherry

½ cup canned coconut milk

2 tablespoons unsalted butter

Rinse the mushrooms briefly under cold water and pat dry with a towel; trim the bottoms of the mushroom stems.

Heat the olive oil in a sauté pan over medium-high heat until the oil barely starts to smoke.

Slide the pan off the heat and carefully add the mushrooms (they may be slightly damp, and that could create spatter).

Return the pan to the burner and cook the mushrooms until they start to color a little, then add the thyme and a pinch each of salt and pepper.

Move the pan off the heat again and pour in the sherry, then carefully return the pan to the burner. This could create a small flambé, so be ready to share a social media story. If it does flame up, simply let the flame dissipate; the alcohol will burn off, leaving no alcohol in the finished dish.

When the sherry is almost gone, reduce the heat to medium-low and pour in the coconut milk. Swirl the pan to coat the mushrooms.

Remove the pan from the heat. Allow to cool for 3 to 5 minutes, then swirl in the butter to coat the mushrooms. Remove the thyme sprigs and serve.

EGGPLANT

Eggplant is a member of the nightshade family, which makes this vegetable sound like it's involved in the seedy world of organized produce crime. (Also, yes, technically it's a fruit, but it tastes and behaves like a vegetable.) Potatoes, tomatoes, and peppers are nightshades. We'd argue they all taste good together too, and that's no coincidence. Things that grow together go together.

Nightshades aren't for everyone, though; some say that they can be pro-inflammatory. For any food sensitivity, we think you should eat it and see how you feel. Alternatively, you can remove that food from your diet for a month or two and then slowly add it back in to see how your body handles it. It's definitely a personal choice, and we choose to eat nightshades because eggplant and tomato sauce are the main components of eggplant Parmesan!

Eggplant, with its deep purple color, is rich in phytonutrients that promote good health. Not to mention it is a great source of fiber, potassium, and magnesium. Fiber makes you feel full and satiated after a meal, and it's clutch for people trying to manage their weight and health. More fiber means less overeating! We're bringing eggplant back to center stage, as more people should be working with this fantastic ingredient.

Eggplant plays a key role for many people who are trying to eat a more plant-based diet. Its fleshy meatiness substitutes seamlessly for chicken in the classic parmigiana. And who doesn't love eggplant when it's breaded and sopping in tomato sauce and mozzarella? Its soft texture yields to creaminess and makes it a perfect replacement for a juicy, flaky fish fillet. And, most importantly, eggplant is mysteriously delicious, featuring notes of bitterness, the most underrated flavor out there—a bitterness that complements many sweet additions, from honey to just-cooked tomatoes.

We'll never understand why more home cooks don't reach for eggplant early and often. It is a very forgiving ingredient. It's the type of food that is as good when perfectly just-cooked as it is when absolutely overcooked, sometimes even intentionally. As a matter of fact, I learned what was probably one of my most important lessons as a cook from overcooking eggplant. Having left an eggplant on the grill for way too long and faced with the thought of throwing it in the garbage or testing the limits of burnt eggplant, I chose the latter. I've tossed many burnt vegetables into the food processor to see what I could make of them. In the case of eggplant (and many others), it becomes the base of a wonderful schmear, spread, topping, or dressing.

Give eggplant a chance; it's a valuable asset in your garden and should be on every plant-forward cook's roster.

The recipes in this chapter often vaguely call for "eggplant," but if you've visited your local farmers' market lately, you've likely seen lots of different varietals besides that grocery store behemoth. Use what you like here—fairy tale eggplants, Italian eggplants, Japanese eggplants, the common globe eggplants, any and all will work—and enjoy supporting your local farmers at the same time.

CAPONATA BRUSCHETTA

OPTION

Caponata is a Swiss Army knife of a dish, although it's Sicilian, not Swiss. It is a sweet and sour dish featuring eggplant that almost could be called a savory relish. Have a jar of it on standby in your fridge for everything from a bagel topping to a dip for gluten-free crackers. Here it serves as a bruschetta topping; it's a step up from your basic diced tomatoes and basil, to be sure.

FOR THE CAPONATA

1 large eggplant (about 1 pound)

1 tablespoon extra-virgin olive oil

1 medium yellow onion, chopped

1 stalk celery, diced

2 large cloves garlic, minced

2 pieces jarred roasted red peppers, diced

1 pound Roma tomatoes, seeded and chopped

¼ cup chopped green olives

2 tablespoons capers, drained

2 tablespoons honey or agave nectar

2 tablespoons sherry vinegar

1 teaspoon salt

¼ teaspoon freshly ground black pepper

FOR THE TOASTS

1 baguette

Extra-virgin olive oil

Salt and pepper

2 tablespoons Balsamic Glaze (page 54)

8 to 10 fresh basil leaves, torn

Preheat the oven to 375°F. Line a sheet pan with aluminum foil.

Place the eggplant on the prepared pan and bake for 30 minutes, or until a knife easily slides through the thickest part.

Remove the eggplant from the oven and allow to cool completely, then cut into small chunks. Set aside.

Heat a large skillet or Dutch oven over medium heat. Pour in the olive oil and heat until the oil starts to shimmer and lightly smoke.

Add the onion and celery and sauté until soft and translucent, 2 to 3 minutes. Stir in the garlic and cook, continuing to stir, for 1 minute more.

Mix in the roasted red peppers, tomatoes, olives, capers, honey, vinegar, salt, and pepper until fully incorporated.

Carefully fold in the eggplant, bring the mixture to a gentle simmer, and cook until the liquid has almost entirely evaporated and the vegetables are soft throughout, about 20 minutes. Taste and adjust the seasoning if needed. Allow to cool to room temperature.

While the caponata is cooling, prepare the toasts: Slice the baguette in half lengthwise, drizzle with olive oil, and sprinkle with salt and pepper. Bake until toasted and slightly golden, about 15 minutes.

Top the bread with the caponata, balsamic glaze, and basil. Cut the bread pieces in half to make four manageable pieces and serve.

NOTES

To save time the day of assembly, you can make the caponata up to 3 days ahead. After allowing it to cool, store the caponata in the refrigerator. For best flavor, allow it to come to room temperature before using.

To make this recipe vegan, use agave nectar in the caponata and make the balsamic glaze with a vegan sweetener.

BABA GHANOUSH

Fun to say, easy to cook, and maybe even preferable to its cousin, hummus, in our eyes, this eggplant spread is a perfect condiment and textural addition, and it's vital in a plant-forward fridge. You can use it as a base on a Mediterranean pizza, on a sandwich, in scrambled eggs, as a dip, or in countless other ways. A good condiment game is key to good eating. Don't be afraid to char the eggplant here, which enhances its natural bitterness and takes this flavor accessory to the next level. Serve it with crudités, flatbread, or pita chips for dipping.

2 pounds eggplants (Italian eggplants work best here)

Juice of 2 large lemons

2 tablespoons tahini

2 tablespoons plain Greek yogurt

3 cloves garlic, chopped

⅓ cup extra-virgin olive oil, plus more for drizzling

Salt

½ cup chopped fresh flat-leaf parsley, for garnish

Preheat a grill or grill pan to high heat. Brush the hot grill grates or pan with olive oil, then place the eggplants directly on the grates or in the pan and char on all sides until softened throughout, about 3 minutes per side.

Remove the eggplants from the grill or pan, allow to cool slightly, and peel them; discard the skins and stems.

Place the peeled eggplants in a colander and allow to drain and cool further for 15 to 20 minutes.

Transfer the eggplants to a food processor and add the lemon juice, tahini, yogurt, and garlic; purée until fluffy and uniform. With the blades turning (use low speed if your food processor has variable speeds), slowly drizzle in the olive oil until the dip emulsifies. Season with salt to taste.

Spoon the baba ghanoush into a bowl, drizzle lightly with olive oil, and top with the parsley. Store leftovers in an airtight container in the refrigerator for up to 5 days.

GRILLED EGGPLANT & TOMATO SALAD

SERVES 4

OPTION

Categorize this dish under antipasto—that's where I'd put it if I was writing a menu for a breezy Mediterranean café. Or use it as a spread on some crunchy bread, or as a topping for any grilled protein. The concept of using cooked and then chilled components will take your salad game to the next level, and it happens to be a great use of leftover vegetables as well.

FOR THE GRILLED EGGPLANT

2 large Japanese eggplants, sliced into ½-inch rounds

2 tablespoons olive oil

Salt and pepper

FOR THE DRESSING

(Makes 1½ cups)

1 cup extra-virgin olive oil

⅓ cup red wine vinegar

2 teaspoons Dijon mustard

½ teaspoon honey

2 tablespoons minced shallots

1 clove garlic, minced

1 teaspoon dried oregano leaves

¼ teaspoon red pepper flakes

FOR THE SALAD

2 large heirloom tomatoes, diced

1 cucumber, sliced in half lengthwise, then into ¼-inch half-moons

1 medium red onion, sliced into half-moons

2 tablespoons crumbled feta cheese or plant-based feta

1 cup fresh basil leaves, roughly chopped

¼ cup fresh mint leaves, roughly chopped

To prepare the eggplant, rub the olive oil on all sides of the slices, then season well with salt and pepper. Preheat a grill or grill pan to high heat.

Grill the eggplant rounds on both sides until soft, about 1 minute per side.

To make the dressing, blend or whisk together the olive oil, vinegar, mustard, honey, shallots, garlic, oregano, and red pepper flakes.

Toss the grilled eggplant, tomatoes, cucumber, and onion in ½ to 1 cup of the dressing, depending on how heavily dressed you like your salad. Transfer the salad to a shallow serving bowl and top with the feta, basil, and mint.

Store any leftover dressing in an airtight container in the refrigerator for up to a week.

NOTE
To make this recipe dairy free, use plant-based feta.

EGGPLANT & CHICKPEA SAMOSAS

An elegant party snack or a first course perhaps, this one will have you thinking vegetarian for all of your future crispy-filled hors d'oeuvre trays. We are improving the health quotient of this often deep-fried classic by baking the samosas instead. The pleasantly meaty texture of chickpeas pairs nicely with the creamy eggplant. If you're craving a dip along with the samosas, try Garlic & Mint Yogurt Sauce (page 30).

FOR THE FILLING

1 pound small eggplants

2 teaspoons olive oil

1 cup canned chickpeas, drained and rinsed

2 cloves garlic, minced

½ jalapeño pepper, seeded and finely chopped

1 teaspoon salt

1 teaspoon ground coriander

1 teaspoon ground cumin

1 teaspoon garam masala

¼ teaspoon turmeric powder

2 tablespoons chopped fresh cilantro

16 (8-inch-square) egg roll wrappers

2 teaspoons chopped fresh mint, for garnish

Lemon wedges, for serving

Preheat the oven to 375°F.

Place the eggplants on a nonstick sheet pan and cover with aluminum foil. Bake for 15 to 20 minutes, until a knife easily slides through the thickest part of the largest eggplant.

Remove the pan from the oven. Allow the eggplants to cool slightly, then peel them, discarding the skins and stems. Place in a colander and allow to drain and cool further for 15 to 20 minutes.

Heat the olive oil in a sauté pan over medium-high heat. Add the chickpeas, garlic, jalapeño, salt, and spices and cook for 1 minute, stirring frequently.

Slide the pan off the heat. Fold in the cooked eggplant and cilantro and mash well to a chunky consistency. (You could also use a food processor or immersion blender for this step.) Transfer the filling to a large mixing bowl. Taste and add salt, if necessary. Refrigerate until cool.

Preheat the oven to 450°F. Line a sheet pan with aluminum foil.

Cut the egg roll wrappers into 8 by 4-inch rectangles.

Place 1½ teaspoons of the filling in the center of each rectangle. Brush the edges lightly with water. Fold the bottom-right corner of the rectangle up and over the top of the filling. Fold the bottom-left corner in the same way to form a pocket. Tuck the top corners down over the folds to seal.

Place the samosas on the lined pan. Bake for 15 to 18 minutes, turning about halfway through, until golden brown. Garnish with chopped mint and serve with lemon wedges.

PENNE
WITH EGGPLANT, PESTO, CHILI & FETA

OPTION

It's known in our house that I could eat pasta every day. It's also known in my restaurants that I tend to be a bit of a snob when it comes to classic Italian pasta dishes. Well, I'm working on my issues, as evidenced here. Feta or any other salted cheese adds a pop of salinity and a crumbly texture that pair so well with the chewy noodles. Calabrian chilies in oil lend a little heat and bite to this dish to counterbalance the creamy eggplant and cheese. The pesto is the crowning moment, though, adding a nice herbaceous punch.

1 pound gluten-free or whole-wheat penne pasta

2 tablespoons olive oil

2 cloves garlic, sliced

1 large eggplant (about 1 pound), cubed

1 teaspoon salt

¼ teaspoon freshly ground black pepper

½ cup white wine

1 cup basil pesto

1 tablespoon unsalted butter

1 teaspoon chopped Calabrian chili peppers (packed in oil) or red pepper flakes

1½ cups crumbled feta cheese, for topping

Cook the penne per the package instructions for al dente. Drain and set aside. Do not rinse the pasta.

Heat the olive oil in a large skillet over medium heat. Add the garlic, eggplant, salt, and pepper and sauté until the eggplant has softened, about 5 minutes.

Pour in the wine to deglaze the pan and cook until almost all of the liquid has evaporated. Whisk in the pesto, butter, and chilies. Fold the pasta into the sauce and spoon into serving bowls. Top with the feta and serve.

NOTES
Other cheeses you could use here are ricotta, grated pecorino, or even small chunks of Parmesan.

To make this recipe gluten free, use a gluten-free pasta.

EGGPLANT BRAISED

IN SAKE, WHITE MISO & AGAVE

SERVES **4**

We are dabbling in a restaurant-style vegetarian entrée here, slowly ratcheting up the difficulty level, but only by a notch or two. The eggplant—in this case, the slender Japanese variety—acts almost like a fish fillet in a tasty salty miso marinade punctuated with sweet agave. Serve this as a side dish for an actual fish fillet, alongside a lamb shank, or even as a main plate, perhaps with some steamed rice and pickled vegetables.

5 or 6 large Japanese eggplants (2 to 3 pounds)

1 tablespoon toasted sesame oil, divided

Salt and pepper

2 tablespoons thinly sliced scallions

1 clove garlic, minced

1 teaspoon peeled and minced fresh ginger

2 tablespoons sake

2 tablespoons white miso

1 tablespoon agave nectar

½ teaspoon sambal oelek or red pepper flakes (optional; see Notes)

1 tablespoon chopped fresh basil

1 tablespoon chopped fresh mint

1 tablespoon chopped fresh shiso leaves (see Notes)

Slice the eggplants in half lengthwise.

Warm 1½ teaspoons of the sesame oil in a large heavy-bottomed skillet over medium-high heat. Season the eggplants with salt and pepper and press flesh side down into the pan, working in batches if necessary to avoid crowding the pan. Sear on both sides until softened throughout, about 3 minutes per side. Remove the eggplants from the pan and set aside to drain on paper towels.

Add the remaining 1½ teaspoons of sesame oil, the scallions, garlic, and ginger to the pan and sauté over medium heat for about 1 minute, until the mixture is fragrant.

Add the sake and cook until the sake starts to bubble.

Stir in the miso, agave, and sambal oelek, if using, and stir with a wooden spoon until combined.

Return the eggplants to the pan and gently fold them into the sauce until each is well coated. Cook for another minute or so, until the sauce clings to the eggplants.

Spoon the eggplants onto a large serving platter and top with the chopped herbs.

NOTES

Sambal oelek is a spicy chili sauce that can be found in many larger grocery stores and in Asian markets.

Shiso leaves are a lovely herb commonly used in Japanese cooking. They bring a flavor that falls somewhere between mint and cilantro. Basil is a decent substitute if you can't find shiso in an Asian grocery or other store near you.

MOUSSAKA

OPTION

I was blessed to grow up in an area of New York that featured a global array of cultures. A place where on any given day, you could find a new country's cuisine to explore. A little place called...Long Island. I particularly enjoyed the many Greek restaurants (and still do), from gyro stands and diners to sit-down tablecloth joints. It was there that I found my love for moussaka. It's like a Mediterranean casserole, a different take on lasagna where eggplant plays the role of the noodle layer. It's usually made with lamb, but this version swaps in mushrooms. The spice blend, featuring cinnamon—my favorite underrepresented spice in savory cuisine—always brings to mind lamb for me. I've found that the spices are what make this dish memorable, though, and omitting the lamb keeps it plant based but flavor forward.

2 large eggplants (about 2 pounds)

Olive oil

Salt and pepper

2 tablespoons grapeseed oil

1 large yellow onion, chopped

2 tablespoons minced garlic

16 ounces cremini mushrooms, cleaned, stems trimmed, and finely chopped

1 pound russet potatoes, peeled and finely diced

1 (28-ounce) can crushed tomatoes

½ cup water

1½ teaspoons coconut aminos

½ teaspoon agave nectar

1 teaspoon paprika

¼ teaspoon ground cinnamon

¼ teaspoon ground cloves

Pinch of freshly grated nutmeg

1 bay leaf

1 large egg, beaten

1 bunch fresh flat-leaf parsley, chopped

FOR THE TOPPING

3 large eggs

1½ cups plain Greek yogurt

½ cup grated Parmesan cheese

¼ teaspoon paprika

½ teaspoon salt

¼ teaspoon freshly ground black pepper

Preheat the oven to 425°F. Line a sheet pan with aluminum foil.

Slice the eggplants lengthwise into planks about ½ inch thick. Rub the eggplant slices on all sides with olive oil and season well with salt and pepper. Arrange them in a single layer on the lined pan.

Roast the eggplants for 20 minutes, or until softened throughout. Remove the pan from the oven, cover with another sheet of foil, and set aside.

Lower the oven temperature to 350°F.

Heat a large heavy-bottomed saucepan over medium-high heat. Pour in the grapeseed oil. Add the onion and sauté until translucent, about 3 minutes. Add the garlic and cook, stirring frequently, for another minute. Stir in the mushrooms and cook until browned, about 5 minutes more.

Stir in the potatoes, crushed tomatoes, water, coconut aminos, agave, paprika, cinnamon, cloves, nutmeg, bay leaf, and 1 teaspoon

of salt. Bring to a simmer, then cover, reduce the heat to low, and cook for 30 minutes, stirring occasionally.

After 30 minutes, remove the lid, increase the heat to medium, and cook until most of the liquid has evaporated, leaving a thick stew.

Adjust the salt and pepper to taste and remove the pan from the heat. Set aside to cool slightly, then stir in the beaten egg and the parsley.

Line a 13 by 9-inch baking dish with half of the roasted eggplant slices. Pour the mushroom-tomato mixture over the eggplant and spread evenly. Top with the remaining eggplant slices. Bake for 30 minutes.

Meanwhile, make the topping: Beat together the eggs and yogurt, then stir in the Parmesan and season with the paprika, salt, and pepper.

Remove the baking dish from the oven, pour the topping over the moussaka, and bake for another 30 minutes, until golden brown on top. Let stand for about 5 minutes before serving.

NOTE
To make this recipe vegetarian, use plant-based parmesan.

EGGPLANT PARMESAN

OPTION OPTION

Eggplant Parmesan is, maybe, the poster child of vegetarian cuisine of the 1990s. It's a classic for a reason; even typing about it has me thinking about ordering takeout (I'm in a hotel as I write). I bet they even classified the traditional recipe as a "healthy vegetarian meal." This recipe takes the original, backs off the gluten, and swaps out the deep fryer for a baked option. The additional step of salting the eggplant before cooking removes a good amount of moisture and allows for a nice crisp when baking. Legend says it also tempers the bitterness of eggplant, which can be a barrier for some people when it comes to this purple fruit. Eggplant Parm satisfies everyone and also happens to be a great gateway to other eggplant-based dishes for less adventurous eaters.

2 medium globe eggplants (about 2 pounds)

Salt

2 cups gluten-free breadcrumbs

2 cups grated Parmesan cheese or plant-based parmesan, divided, plus more for garnish

1 tablespoon garlic powder

1 tablespoon onion powder

1 tablespoon dried oregano leaves

4 large eggs

2½ cups no-added-sugar marinara sauce

Leaves from 1 bunch fresh basil

8 ounces shredded mozzarella cheese or vegan mozzarella shreds

Freshly ground black pepper

Red pepper flakes, for serving (optional)

Line a sheet pan with paper towels. Slice the eggplant into ½-inch-thick rounds.

Sprinkle both sides of the eggplant rounds generously with salt and lay them in a single layer on the lined pan. Cover with more paper towels and place a second sheet pan or baking sheet on top to press them lightly. Set aside for 20 minutes to release moisture.

Meanwhile, prepare the breading and egg wash: Combine the breadcrumbs, 1 cup of the Parmesan cheese, and the seasonings in a shallow bowl. In a separate shallow bowl, whisk the eggs.

Preheat the oven to 400°F.

Generously spray a sheet pan with avocado oil cooking spray. Blot the eggplant rounds with paper towels to remove most of the salt and any remaining surface moisture. Dip the eggplant into the whisked eggs, then coat them on all sides in the seasoned bread-crumb mixture, pressing gently to get full coverage. Arrange the coated eggplant rounds in a single layer on the greased pan.

Bake for about 25 minutes, flipping the eggplant once halfway through. Remove from the oven when the eggplant is just golden brown.

To assemble, spread a light layer of the marinara sauce on the bottom of a 13 by 9-inch baking dish; a scant ½ cup should do it.

Place a layer of the eggplant, a few basil leaves, a handful of mozzarella, a generous sprinkling (about ⅓ cup) of the remaining Parmesan cheese, and another ¾ cup of the sauce. Continue layering until all of the eggplant is in the dish, reserving some basil for garnish. Top with the remaining sauce and mozzarella.

Bake until the cheese is melted and bubbling, 10 to 15 minutes. If you like a super crispy top, give it a quick broil at the end.

Remove from the oven and allow to cool slightly before cutting. Top each slice with basil leaves and a sprinkling of Parmesan cheese, salt, pepper, and red pepper flakes, if desired.

NOTES

In traditional recipes for eggplant Parmesan, the eggplant is fried before baking. For this lighter version, par-baking the eggplant slices helps ensure that the eggplant comes out fully cooked in the end.

To make this recipe vegetarian, use plant-based parmesan. To make it dairy free, also use vegan mozzarella shreds.

BROWN RICE
FLOUR

BUCKWHEAT
FLOUR

RED
LENTILS

OATMEAL

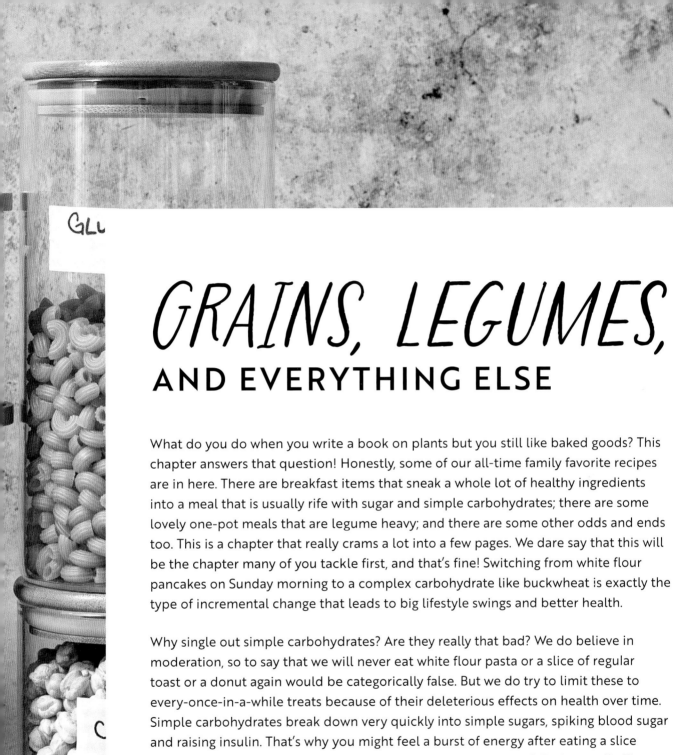

GRAINS, LEGUMES,
AND EVERYTHING ELSE

What do you do when you write a book on plants but you still like baked goods? This chapter answers that question! Honestly, some of our all-time family favorite recipes are in here. There are breakfast items that sneak a whole lot of healthy ingredients into a meal that is usually rife with sugar and simple carbohydrates; there are some lovely one-pot meals that are legume heavy; and there are some other odds and ends too. This is a chapter that really crams a lot into a few pages. We dare say that this will be the chapter many of you tackle first, and that's fine! Switching from white flour pancakes on Sunday morning to a complex carbohydrate like buckwheat is exactly the type of incremental change that leads to big lifestyle swings and better health.

Why single out simple carbohydrates? Are they really that bad? We do believe in moderation, so to say that we will never eat white flour pasta or a slice of regular toast or a donut again would be categorically false. But we do try to limit these to every-once-in-a-while treats because of their deleterious effects on health over time. Simple carbohydrates break down very quickly into simple sugars, spiking blood sugar and raising insulin. That's why you might feel a burst of energy after eating a slice of cake, but the crash comes on quickly once your blood sugar falls drastically. The long-term effects of repeatedly spiking blood sugar include late-onset diabetes, heart problems, kidney problems, neuropathy, and a cascade of other health issues. Although simple carbohydrates are not the only villain, they are one to steer clear of for health purposes.

Enter complex carbohydrates. Our bodies digest complex carbohydrates more slowly, so insulin levels do not jump as high. They also have more fiber, so they keep you full longer, leading to fewer instances of overeating. A great tip we received from a nutritionist is that if we never feel satiated by a particular snack, it is probably not nutritionally diverse enough. It's too simple. Complex carbs like whole grains and legumes are great ways to diversify your recipes (and snacking) and increase their nutritional content instantly.

Whole grains are edible seeds harvested from grass. They are, plainly, grains that are not refined or processed into some simpler form—for example, whole-wheat flour versus white flour (which removes the germ and bran from the wheat grain). Undoubtedly, the parts that are removed are the healthiest parts that contain the fiber, vitamins, fat, and protein. This holds true for brown rice and white rice as well as whole-grain pasta versus white flour pasta, which is why we endorse whole-grain or gluten-free pasta (which is often made from legumes) throughout this book. Some of our other favorite whole grains are oatmeal, buckwheat, and quinoa.

We aren't following the Paleo diet, and we aren't saying grains are bad. Everything in moderation applies as always. However, choosing whole grains most of the time will have a dynamic effect on your health, your waistline, and your satiety at mealtimes.

In this chapter, and dotted throughout the recipes in this book, you'll see that we turn to nuts to provide nutrition, density, and texture. We also use nut flours and nut milks to replace traditional wheat flour and dairy milk to keep a recipe gluten free or dairy free. Nuts are high in fiber, protein, and omega-3 fatty acids. They are extremely versatile and can be drunk in a smoothie, made into cheese, or baked into a cake. Enjoy them in moderation because they are nutritionally dense and definitely add a caloric load that needs to be considered when meal planning. Also, when buying premade nut butters and nut milks, check the labels for any added ingredients—avoid the ones with lots of added sugar, gums, and preservatives.

Legumes—a pretty wide and diverse category of vegetables—are grown all over the world. Peanuts aren't the only legume, although they might be the poster child. Legumes are the seeds of plants and are eaten in their immature form, which is why there are a lot of beans in this category. The workhorses of the group are beans like black beans and fava beans, but don't forget about chickpeas, lentils, green peas, and more. Sixteen thousand more, to be accurate.

Legumes differ from their mature vegetable plant counterparts in that they are packed with fiber, starch, and protein—the building blocks of life that a seed needs to start a healthy plant. They can lower cholesterol, decrease blood sugar, and improve gut health, and they are extremely versatile, as you'll see in the following pages with recipes like Chickpea "Tuna" Salad (page 256).

This chapter is the gateway to healthy eating for those who are resistant to a book called *Plant Forward*. Some people legitimately don't like vegetables, but maybe they like legumes. Even if you choose one day a week to start making healthier choices, that's a big change. You may even notice that you have more energy on those days and that you sleep better at night, or you wake up the next day feeling great. That will lead to better choices and more gains, we're sure of it.

So swap out that flour tortilla for corn, switch the white flour for almond flour, and fill your plate with complex, delicious, and nutritious foods!

BANANA PANCAKES

SERVES

4

OPTION   OPTION

I am a fan of bananas. There are times when I eat at least one a day. I find them satisfying before a workout or run or as a quick bite for breakfast. So we always have a bunch in the house, and sometimes we have a few that are a little overripe—not so overripe that they could be banana bread, but yellow-with-lots-of-brown-spots ripe. If you find yourself in the same position, these pancakes are the perfect solution: not only are they a delicious breakfast treat that the whole family will enjoy, but they come together quickly in a blender and also store well (up to a month in the freezer or four days in the fridge).

FOR THE BATTER

2 medium-sized ripe bananas

2 large eggs

½ cup plain unsweetened almond milk

1 teaspoon vanilla extract

1½ cups old-fashioned oats

2 teaspoons baking powder

½ teaspoon ground cinnamon

¼ teaspoon salt

Ghee, for the pan

FOR SERVING

Butter (see Note)

Sliced banana

Maple syrup

Preheat a griddle pan over medium heat.

Place all of the ingredients for the batter in the order listed in a blender. Blend for 30 seconds, or just until the batter becomes uniform. You can blend until it's smooth or leave some texture from the oats (I prefer the latter).

Melt 1 tablespoon of ghee, or more if needed, on the griddle, using enough to cover the entire surface. Pour 4-inch rounds of batter directly from the blender onto the hot pan, leaving a few inches of space between them for easier flipping. Cook for about 2 minutes, until the edges are set and lightly browned, then flip and cook the other side until lightly browned, about 2 minutes more.

Repeat with the remaining batter, adding more ghee to the griddle as needed. You should get about 8 pancakes.

Serve with butter, sliced banana, and maple syrup.

NOTE
To make this recipe dairy free, omit the butter or use a plant-based alternative. Make sure to grab oats that are labeled gluten free if avoiding gluten is important to you.

BUCKWHEAT PANCAKES

WITH KEFIR, BANANA & SPROUTED WALNUTS

It's safe to say that I am the only person in our family who likes this recipe. In fact, the girls call them "butt wheat" pancakes, which is absolute Blaisphemy. I, however, love them so much and love that they are whole grain and gluten free, so I had to include them in this book. Buckwheat is earthy in a good way, and it pairs so well with the sour-sweet kefir and banana. I top these pancakes with some keto maple syrup that Jazmin orders online. I'm genuinely interested if people will love these pancakes like I do. Shoot me a DM if you are Team Buckwheat.

FOR THE BATTER

1 large egg

1 cup buckwheat flour

1 teaspoon baking powder

1 teaspoon baking soda

Pinch of salt

¾ cup plain kefir, plus more if needed

2 tablespoons unsalted butter, melted and cooled

Ghee or avocado oil cooking spray, for the pan

FOR TOPPING

Butter (optional)

Maple syrup (optional)

Sliced banana

Sprouted Walnuts (page 48)

In a medium-sized mixing bowl, whisk the egg.

In a small bowl, whisk together the flour, baking powder, baking soda, and salt.

Add the kefir and melted butter to the egg and whisk. Fold in the dry ingredients and mix until the wet and dry ingredients are combined with few lumps, if any. You should have a perfect pancake batter consistency, thick but pourable; if it's too thick, adjust with more kefir.

While the batter rests, preheat a griddle pan over medium heat. This will give the buckwheat flour a little extra time to hydrate.

Grease the hot griddle with a little ghee or cooking spray and, working in batches, spoon the batter onto the pan to form 3- to 4-inch rounds, leaving room for flipping.

When the batter starts to set around the edges and the underside is lightly browned, flip the pancakes and cook the other side for another 2 to 3 minutes, until lightly browned on both sides. Remove and repeat with the remaining batter, adding more cooking spray to the griddle as needed. You should get a total of 10 to 12 pancakes.

If desired, top each pancake with a little butter, a drizzle of maple syrup, and a scattering of sliced banana and walnuts. If you're being more calorie conscious, they're perfectly delicious with just banana slices.

COCONUT PANCAKES

OPTION

So, if you're not team buckwheat pancakes, it's pretty much guaranteed that you'll be team coconut pancakes. These are classic pancakes with a tropical twist, plus they're dairy free (assuming you use coconut yogurt) and gluten free. They're tasty topped with butter and syrup, or you can really amp up the island paradise vibes and go with sliced bananas, toasted shredded coconut, coconut butter, and crushed macadamia nuts. The thing I love about this recipe is its flexibility. Don't have coconut yogurt and don't mind a little dairy? Use regular yogurt, sour cream, or even cottage cheese! Don't be afraid to substitute LIKE with LIKE to make your LIFE easier.

FOR THE BATTER

¾ cup plain coconut yogurt or whole-milk plain Greek yogurt

½ cup nondairy milk

1 large egg

¼ teaspoon vanilla extract

⅛ teaspoon pure powdered stevia

¾ cup all-purpose gluten-free flour

1 teaspoon baking powder

½ teaspoon baking soda

¼ teaspoon salt

¼ teaspoon ground cinnamon

Pinch of freshly grated nutmeg

Ghee, for the pan

FOR TOPPING

Coconut butter, warmed just until liquidy

Sliced bananas

Unsweetened shredded coconut, toasted (see Note)

Chopped macadamia nuts

Preheat a griddle pan over medium heat.

In a medium-sized mixing bowl, combine the yogurt, milk, egg, vanilla, and stevia.

In a small bowl, whisk together the flour, baking powder, baking soda, salt, and spices.

Add one-third of the dry mixture at a time to the wet and stir to incorporate, continuing until all of the ingredients are just combined. Do not overmix.

Let the batter sit for a few minutes. You should see some bubbles form; this is a good sign of fluffy pancakes ahead.

While the batter is resting, prepare the toppings.

Grease the hot griddle with ghee. Working in batches, drop the batter ⅓ cup at a time into rounds evenly spaced on the pan, leaving room for flipping. Once the edges of the pancakes look set and bubbles have formed on the surface, flip to brown the other side for another 3 to 4 minutes. Remove and repeat with the remaining batter, adding more ghee to the griddle as needed. You should get a total of 6 to 8 pancakes.

Serve warm, topped with a drizzle of warmed coconut butter, banana slices, toasted coconut shreds, and chopped macadamia nuts.

NOTE
To toast shredded coconut, heat a small skillet over medium heat; put the coconut in the pan and toast, moving the pan continuously, until golden brown, 3 to 5 minutes. Remove from the pan immediately to avoid burning.

PETIT POIS-CAMOLE

(FROZEN PEA GUACAMOLE)

MORE PUNS! Now in French! This recipe is categorically somewhere between a guacamole and a hummus, but I dare you to serve it and not tell a soul there are peas in there. No one would be able to put their finger on that certain je ne sais quoi. The avocado and olive oil give the peas a bit of healthy fat and a creamy texture, and the peas give the avocado dip a lot more fiber. Use this for chips or even as a sandwich spread.

1 ripe avocado

2 cups frozen green peas, defrosted

½ teaspoon ground cumin

¼ teaspoon ground coriander

1 tablespoon extra-virgin olive oil

1 tablespoon seeded and finely chopped jalapeño pepper

1 tablespoon chopped fresh cilantro

2 teaspoons chopped fresh dill

½ teaspoon chopped fresh tarragon

1 teaspoon dried mint

Salt and pepper

Juice of ½ lime

Slice the avocado in half, rotating the knife around the pit and twisting the two halves to open. Remove the pit and use a spoon to scoop the flesh from the shell. Set the flesh aside.

In a food processor fitted with the blade attachment, pulse the peas, cumin, coriander, and olive oil until the peas are roughly chopped. Add the avocado, jalapeño, and all of the herbs and pulse for 5 to 10 seconds so the mixture is roughly chopped but also creamy.

Transfer to a bowl and season with salt and pepper to taste. Add the lime juice and mix well.

Serve immediately or chill for 2 hours before serving.

CHICKPEA "TUNA" SALAD

This is one of my favorite plant-based recipes, and it was a staple in our home during the Covid quarantine. It's a chickpea salad that will remind you of tuna. Honestly, you can make this for someone who loves tuna salad sandwiches, and they won't guess it's chickpeas. At this point, we actually prefer this version to the real deal, and we think you will too. A food processor comes in handy here as it does for many dips and spreads in a plant-based arsenal.

1 (15-ounce) can chickpeas, drained and rinsed

¼ cup Sprouted Walnuts (page 48) or raw walnuts

½ cup avocado oil mayonnaise

1 tablespoon prepared yellow mustard

Juice of ½ lemon

1 scant tablespoon extra-virgin olive oil, plus more if needed

1 teaspoon red wine vinegar

1 tablespoon capers, drained

½ teaspoon curry powder

½ teaspoon garlic powder

3 tablespoons finely diced white onions

2 tablespoons sliced celery

2 tablespoons chopped cornichons

1 tablespoon chopped fresh dill, plus more for garnish

Salt and pepper

Butter or Bibb lettuce leaves, washed and dried, for serving

6 to 8 fresh parsley leaves, torn, for garnish

In a food processor, pulse the chickpeas, walnuts, mayo, mustard, lemon juice, olive oil, vinegar, capers, curry power, and garlic powder until the mixture has a tuna salad–like consistency, adding more oil if needed to help the process.

Transfer the mixture to a medium-sized mixing bowl and fold in the onions, celery, cornichons, and dill. Season with salt and pepper to taste.

Lay out the lettuce cups and fill each one with about ½ cup of "tuna" salad. Sprinkle some chopped dill and torn parsley over the top of each lettuce cup and serve.

NOTES

This recipe is very flexible—make it yours! Try garnishing with a splash of hot sauce. Or swap out the dill for cilantro or basil and add a little grated ginger.

To make this recipe vegan, use vegan mayo.

AVOCADO MAC SALAD

OPTION

I consider myself a bit of an aficionado of macaroni salad, or mac salad as it's known on the islands of Hawaii. The whole family loves it. Given our love of Hawaii, pasta, and mayonnaise, this popular cookout side has been ever-present in our lives. Now, I say all this because I don't want you to hate me for having made this version a bit lighter and healthier. I've swapped in gluten-free elbows for regular pasta—there are some really good ones in this shape—and avocado and yogurt for the mayo. I even added cilantro to make it really controversial. Crazy? Maybe, but I love it.

1 ripe avocado, pitted

¼ cup plain Greek yogurt

3 tablespoons plain kefir

3 tablespoons apple cider vinegar

1 tablespoon honey

2 teaspoons prepared yellow mustard

3 tablespoons diced celery

1 tablespoon grated white onion

1 tablespoon salt

1 teaspoon dried chives

1 teaspoon dried parsley

1 teaspoon garlic powder

2 tablespoons chopped fresh cilantro (optional)

2 cups cooked gluten-free or whole-wheat elbow macaroni

Scoop the avocado flesh into a large mixing bowl. Add the yogurt and mash until smooth. You could use a food processor here, but I'm trying to save you dishes; mashing by hand takes a bit more time, but you can do it!

Add the remaining ingredients, except the macaroni, to the avocado mixture and whisk to combine.

Gently fold the cooked macaroni into the dressing. Refrigerate for at least an hour before serving.

NOTE
To make this recipe gluten free, use a gluten-free pasta.

GRILLED CORN SALAD

WITH COTIJA & JALAPEÑO

Fun fact: When you eat corn on the cob, it's considered a vegetable, but when the kernels are cut off the cob, they're considered a whole grain! So, while this technically qualifies as a grain salad, it isn't overly heavy. Quite the contrary, it's light and fun with a good spicy kick from the jalapeño. Serve it alongside some barbecued ribs or a nice piece of grilled salmon for dinner and you'll be fully satisfied.

4 ears corn, husks removed

1 tablespoon olive oil

Salt and pepper

¼ cup plain Greek yogurt

3 tablespoons avocado oil mayonnaise

2 tablespoons Cotija cheese crumbles

1 tablespoon chopped fresh cilantro

1 tablespoon sliced scallions

1 small jalapeño pepper, seeded and finely chopped

1 teaspoon Tajin seasoning (see Note)

Preheat a grill to medium-high heat.

Brush the corn with the olive oil and season with a good sprinkling of salt and pepper.

Grill the corn, turning occasionally, until half of the kernels are light brown.

Remove the corn from the grill and let it cool slightly, then shave the kernels off the cobs into a bowl.

Add the remaining ingredients to the bowl and mix to combine with the corn.

NOTE

Tajin is a super-easy-to-find Mexican spice blend comprised of chili powder, lime, and salt. You can find recipes online for making it yourself, but it's easier to use a ready-made version.

BLISTERED SNAP PEAS

WITH FETA & MINT

I love this recipe so much that you'll undoubtedly see a version of it on any menu I write. You could switch out the cheese for a dairy-free alternative or use salted ricotta instead, but the classic brininess of feta here really makes my day.

½ cup avocado oil mayonnaise

½ cup plain Greek yogurt

2 teaspoons hot paprika

Juice of 1 lemon, divided

2 tablespoons ghee

1 pound snap peas, trimmed

¼ cup loosely packed fresh mint leaves

½ cup crumbled feta cheese

In a medium-sized mixing bowl, stir together the mayonnaise, yogurt, paprika, and half of the lemon juice. Set aside.

Heat a large heavy-bottomed skillet over high heat, then melt the ghee in the pan. Add the snap peas and sear on one side for 30 seconds to 1 minute. When done, the underside of the peas will be blistered and will have just started to blacken in spots. Cook the peas for another 30 seconds, tossing intermittently.

Immediately add the peas to the bowl of sauce and stir to coat. Fold in the mint.

Serve topped with the feta and the remaining lemon juice.

SUMMER VEGETABLE SUCCOTASH

SERVES 4

OPTION   OPTION

A delicious and nutritious meal can come from the budget bin, a can, or the frozen food section. Hopefully you have picked up by now that although we love to eat vegetables and clearly are encouraging a healthy diet, we aren't telling you the only way to do it is from the farmers' market. For budget's sake, you could just as easily use frozen lima beans and canned corn for this recipe, and it will turn out just fine. But for honesty's sake, this deep summer succotash was inspired when we visited Chino Farms in Rancho Santa Fe, California, a world-class farm that supplies ingredients to some of the country's best restaurants. We came home with summer's greatest hits—favas, corn, and tomatoes—and whipped up this quick take on succotash straightaway. We chose favas because they're such a special find in summer and their texture is a bit more delicate than limas. If you're not a fan of cilantro, basil, parsley, or tarragon would also work well.

1 cup shelled broad beans, such as favas or limas (fresh, canned, or frozen)

1 teaspoon olive oil

1½ teaspoons finely diced shallots or white onions

¼ cup finely diced red bell peppers

½ cup cherry tomatoes, halved

2 ears corn, husked and kernels cut off cobs, or 1 cup frozen corn kernels

1 tablespoon chopped fresh cilantro

1 tablespoon unsalted butter

1½ teaspoons grated Parmesan or Cotija cheese (optional)

Juice of 1 lemon or lime wedge

Salt and pepper

If the beans are fresh from the market, boil them in a pot of salted water for 3 minutes, then drain and set aside. If you are using canned beans, simply drain and rinse them. If using frozen beans, you can use them directly from the freezer, no need to defrost.

In a sauté pan, warm the olive oil over medium heat. Add the shallots and cook until translucent, 2 to 3 minutes. If using frozen beans, add them to the pan now.

Add the bell peppers to the pan and continue to cook for a few minutes, until they just soften and become fragrant.

If using boiled or canned beans, add them to the pan along with the tomatoes, then toss with the shallots and bell peppers and cook until the tomatoes begin to soften and wrinkle, about 2 minutes more.

Reduce the heat to low and stir in the corn. Cook for 1 minute more, or until the corn becomes glassy. If using frozen corn, cook until it is warmed through.

Remove the pan from the heat and mix in the cilantro, butter, cheese (if using), and citrus juice. Season with salt and pepper to taste.

MULLIGATAWNY STEW

A favorite South Indian stew with a British twist that's easy to make and even easier to devour. This version has lentils, sweet potato, apple, and fresh cilantro, and we've added plenty of kale to the classic rendition. As is the case with a lot of stews, you could pour this over a bowl of brown rice or serve it with some warm flatbread and have a proper filling dinner.

2 tablespoons ghee

1 medium yellow onion, diced

2 celery stalks, finely diced

1 carrot, peeled and finely diced

1½ tablespoons curry powder

1 pound boneless, skinless chicken thighs or lamb shoulder or stew meat, cut into ½-inch chunks

Salt

Ground white pepper

2 tablespoons tomato paste

1 quart low-sodium chicken stock

2 cups plain unsweetened coconut milk

1 small sweet potato (about 8 ounces), scrubbed and finely diced

¼ cup dried lentils

2 cups destemmed and roughly chopped kale

1 green apple, finely diced

FOR GARNISH/SERVING

¼ cup chopped fresh cilantro leaves

Juice of ½ lime (optional)

Hot sauce (optional)

Heat the ghee in a heavy-bottomed saucepot. Add the onion, celery, carrot, and curry powder and sweat over medium-low heat for 3 to 5 minutes, until the onion is translucent.

Season the meat with salt and pepper and add to the pot, cooking for 3 to 5 minutes a side, until browned.

Stir in the tomato paste with a wooden spoon. Allow to cook for an additional 2 minutes.

Pour in the stock and coconut milk and stir, scraping any cooked bits from the bottom of the pot. Stir in the sweet potato and lentils and bring to a gentle simmer. Cook for 45 minutes for chicken or up to 1 hour 15 minutes if using lamb. The internal temperature of the lamb should be a minimum of 145°F when a thermometer is inserted in its thickest part.

Turn off the heat. Taste the stew and adjust the seasoning with salt and pepper. Fold in the kale and apple and let sit in the hot stew to soften for 10 minutes before serving.

Top with the chopped cilantro and, if desired, lime juice and hot sauce.

SIMPLE CHANA MASALA

I've long been curious why Indian cuisine hasn't achieved the mass commercial success that, say, Mexican cuisine or Japanese sushi has over the last few decades. Indian food in general is heavily plant focused, elegantly spiced, and vibrantly colored and ticks all of the health, wellness, and deliciousness checkboxes. I love the cuisine, which can be hyper-regional and vast. Now, I know this is a training wheels, 101-style dish, but it's one we eat often as a side or as a component of a vegetable bowl. Serve it over a bed of brown rice, or opt for cauliflower rice for extra nutrient density!

1 tablespoon ghee

1 medium yellow onion, diced

½ jalapeño pepper, seeded and finely chopped

5 cloves garlic, grated

2 tablespoons peeled and grated fresh ginger

1 tablespoon cumin seeds, or 2½ teaspoons ground cumin

1 tablespoon garam masala

1½ teaspoons chili powder

1½ teaspoons ground coriander

1 teaspoon turmeric powder

2 cups tomato puree

1 cup diced tomatoes, fresh or canned, with juices

2 tablespoons finely chopped dried mango (optional; see Note)

1 large russet potato, cubed

2 (15-ounce) cans chickpeas, drained and rinsed

1 cup frozen green peas

¼ cup chopped fresh cilantro

Melt the ghee in a large cast-iron or other heavy-bottomed skillet over medium-high heat, then add the onion, jalapeño, garlic, and ginger and sauté for a few minutes, until fragrant.

Add the spices and cook while stirring for an additional minute.

Deglaze the pan by adding the tomato puree and diced tomatoes and scraping the bottom of the pan with a wooden spoon to remove any crispy bits and spices. Add the mango, if using, and stir to combine. Bring to a gentle simmer and simmer for 10 minutes.

Add the potato. Cover and cook for 10 minutes, or until the potato has softened, then add the chickpeas and frozen green peas and stir to combine. Cook for a few more minutes, until the green peas are plump and warm. Remove from the heat and stir in the cilantro.

NOTE

Dried mango is the more readily available substitute for amchoor, a powder made from green mangoes that is used often in Indian cuisine. Dried mango can be found at most grocery stores, such as Trader Joe's and Costco. It adds sweetness and depth to this dish, plus a bit of vitamin C.

BAKED FALAFEL

It's arguably the poster dish of vegetarian snack fare and street food, but falafel is so much more. Falafel works stuffed into a pita, as an accompaniment to a salad bowl, or on a tray passed as a fancy hors d'oeuvre! It's the perfect food to start getting away from less-healthy fried and fast food, and it wins over vegetarians and omnivores alike. We took this recipe one step further into healthy territory by baking instead of deep-frying the falafel so it's that much better for you. This version uses dried chickpeas (aka garbanzo beans), which take twenty-four hours to soak, but we think the authenticity of doing it the traditional way pays off. Can you make this with canned chickpeas? Yes, but you'd be trading that beautiful crumbly texture of classic falafel for a mushier one because of the wetness of canned chickpeas.

1¾ cups dried chickpeas

Cold filtered water, for soaking

1 cup roughly chopped fresh cilantro

½ cup roughly chopped fresh parsley

4 cloves garlic, smashed with the side of a knife

1 tablespoon lemon juice

1 tablespoon ground cumin

1 teaspoon ground coriander

1 teaspoon salt

½ teaspoon freshly ground black pepper

½ teaspoon baking soda

Olive oil, for the pan

FOR GARNISH/SERVING

Chopped fresh parsley or cilantro

Garlic & Mint Yogurt Sauce (page 30)

Lemon wedges

Soak the chickpeas in a bowl of cold filtered water in the refrigerator for 24 hours, then drain and rinse.

In a meat grinder or food processor, pulse or grind the chickpeas, cilantro, parsley, and garlic until the chickpeas are granular but not pastelike.

Transfer the mixture to a medium-sized mixing bowl, add the remaining ingredients, and stir to combine.

Using your hands or an ice cream scoop, form the chickpea mixture into golf ball–sized balls and place on a sheet pan lined with parchment paper. Refrigerate for at least 1 hour or up to 4 hours to allow the balls to firm up.

After the falafel have rested, preheat the oven to 350°F and remove the pan from the fridge.

Drizzle a generous amount of olive oil on a separate sheet pan—3 to 4 tablespoons should do it. Place the pan in the oven and allow it to heat up for 5 minutes.

Pull the hot oiled pan out of the oven and arrange the falafel on it, leaving a few inches of space between them for easier turning.

Bake for 30 minutes, turning the falafel every 10 minutes to brown on all sides. They should be warm in the center and golden brown on the outside. Add additional cooking time if needed.

Remove the pan from the oven and allow the falafel to cool for a few minutes before transferring them to a bowl or serving plate.

Garnish with a scattering of parsley or cilantro and serve with yogurt sauce and lemon wedges.

MANGO STICKY "RICE" CHIA PUDDING

For all you keto fans, this recipe is grain free and brimming with healthy fat and fiber. This is the kind of snack that satisfies a sweet tooth and also hunger. Traditional mango sticky rice can often be found at your local Thai spot, but the original version includes lots of sugar. Plus, if you're trying to limit your grain intake, the original dish is off-limits. Made with chia seeds, this nod is satiating, and you won't feel an ounce of regret for the indulgence.

1 (13.5-ounce) can coconut milk

½ cup chia seeds

1 teaspoon vanilla extract

⅛ to ¼ teaspoon powdered stevia, depending on desired level of sweetness

2 ripe mangoes, peeled and diced

Put the coconut milk, chia seeds, vanilla, and stevia in a medium-sized glass bowl and stir well.

Cover, place the bowl in the fridge, and let the chia seeds hydrate for at least 4 hours or overnight for best results.

Serve cold topped with the diced mangoes.

ANYTIME ALMOND BISCUITS

OPTION

My friend and world traveler Simon Majumdar introduced this recipe to me, and I've since added a few fold-ins of my own. It's a great gluten-free breakfast option with some natural jam and butter, or you can easily make it savory by folding cheese and chives into the dough and filling the biscuits with prosciutto. I've given you both sweet and savory options here. Any which way, it's a winner.

2 large eggs

5 tablespoons unsalted butter or ghee, melted and cooled

2 cups blanched almond flour

1½ teaspoons baking powder

½ teaspoon salt

FOR THE SWEET OPTION

½ teaspoon almond extract

Unsalted butter, room temperature

Wild Blueberry Chia Jam (page 44)

FOR THE SAVORY OPTION

2 tablespoons shredded cheddar cheese or vegan cheddar

1 tablespoon chopped fresh chives

Unsalted butter, room temperature

Thinly sliced prosciutto (1 slice per biscuit)

Preheat the oven to 375°F. Spray a baking sheet with ghee cooking spray.

In a medium-sized mixing bowl, whisk the eggs until very frothy. Whisk the cooled melted butter into the frothy eggs. If making the sweet option, whisk in the almond extract.

In a separate medium-sized mixing bowl, whisk together the almond flour, baking powder, and salt.

Using your hands or a rubber spatula, incorporate the dry ingredients into the wet and work to a loose paste. If you are going the savory route, fold in the cheese and chives.

Using a spoon or scoop, drop a little less than ½ cup of dough per biscuit onto the greased baking sheet, leaving 3 inches of space between biscuits. You should get a total of 6 biscuits. Bake until the edges and tops are golden brown, 20 to 25 minutes. Allow to cool on the pan for 10 minutes, then serve warm or transfer to a wire rack to finish cooling.

To serve, gently slice each biscuit in half. For the sweet version, add a pat of butter and a spoonful of jam to the warm middle. For the savory preparation, smear the top and bottom with butter and sandwich a slice of prosciutto in each biscuit.

NOTE
To make this recipe vegetarian, prepare the sweet option.

THE GRAIN-FREE COOKIE

OPTION   OPTION

Jazmin has long been on a quest to make the perfect grain-free cookie. There have been many versions, but this one is the winner. It's soft with a little chew, and the sweetness level is perfect. Use your favorite chocolate bar or chocolate chips to really personalize the experience.

½ cup vanilla-flavored protein powder

½ teaspoon baking soda

¼ teaspoon salt

¾ cup nut or seed butter of choice

1 to 2 tablespoons coconut oil, melted (see Notes)

⅓ cup unsweetened applesauce

1½ tablespoons maple syrup or coconut nectar

¼ teaspoon vanilla extract

⅓ cup stevia-sweetened chocolate chips or chopped chocolate bar

Preheat the oven to 350°F. Line a baking sheet with parchment paper.

In a small mixing bowl, whisk together the protein powder, baking soda, and salt.

In a large mixing bowl, whisk together the nut butter, melted coconut oil, applesauce, maple syrup, and vanilla until well incorporated.

Add the dry ingredients to the wet and stir with a wooden spoon. The dough will be thick. Fold in the chocolate chips.

Using a 3-tablespoon cookie scoop or a large spoon, make 8 rounded mounds of dough on the prepared baking sheet, spacing them about 2 inches apart. Place the pan in the fridge for at least 15 minutes for the dough to set. Remove from the fridge and, using the flat bottom of a glass or jar, press the dough until it's about an inch thick. The cookies will not spread much once flattened.

Bake the cookies for 10 minutes, or until the edges look set and slightly golden brown. Remove to a wire rack to cool for 15 minutes before eating. Enjoy warm. Store at room temperature for up to 3 days.

NOTES

The amount of coconut oil you need will depend on how thick your nut butter is. If it runs easily off a spoon, use 1 tablespoon of coconut oil; if it is thick and not runny, use 2 tablespoons.

To make this recipe dairy free, use a protein powder that does not contain whey. To make it vegan, use a vegan protein powder.

ACKNOWLEDGMENTS ─────────

From Richard:

This book, at some point, was called "My wife saved my life," and it still is to me internally and eternally. There was a time on a hill in Piedmont Park, Atlanta, where my eyes were filled with tears, my bank account empty—negative, actually—and my physical, emotional, and mental state was, at best, on edge. You, Jazmin, decided to stick by my side not during the best of times, but the most uncertain of them. Your unwavering support and invaluable contribution to my journey and our family's toward a healthier and happier life will never be lost on me.

Jazmin, you have been my guiding light, my rock, and my inspiration throughout this long, arduous, and transformative process. Your belief in me, even when I doubted myself, even as I doubt myself still, has been nothing short of remarkable. Your love and encouragement, and indeed sometimes no-nonsense approach, have propelled me forward, pushing me to explore new avenues and embrace a better understanding of health and wellness even if I don't listen to all of the podcasts or open up all of the links.

Your extensive knowledge and passion for health and wellness have been a lifeline for me, and knowing your work on this book creates that potential lifeline for others solidifies you as the angel you are.

You have tirelessly researched and shared valuable information, guiding me toward making informed choices and adopting healthier habits. Your dedication to understanding the intricacies of nutrition, exercise, and mental well-being has not only saved my life but also enriched it in countless ways.

Beyond your expertise, it is your unwavering support and understanding that have truly made a difference. You have been my confidante, my sounding board, my tough trainer, my guru, always there to lend an empathetic ear or offer a gentle—OK, strong-handed—nudge in the right direction. Your patience and understanding during the challenging moments, like that hill in Atlanta, all of the restaurant and TV struggles, and quite honestly any random Tuesday, have been a constant reminder of the strength of our bond, a bond I'm so happy to share further with the world in this book.

I am eternally grateful for the sacrifices you have made to ensure my well-being and our family's. From preparing nutritious meals to encouraging me to prioritize self-care, you have consistently gone above and beyond to ensure that we are on the path to optimal health. Your selflessness and dedication have not gone unnoticed, and even our kids will one day realize this ;)

I am excited to continue exploring the boundless possibilities that lie ahead on our journey together. With your love and support, I am confident that we will continue to grow, learn, and thrive in our pursuit of a healthier and more fulfilling life.

Thank you, Jazmin, for being my guiding light not only within the confines of this book, but in the journey of life. You have truly saved my life, and I am forever grateful.

Oh, would you like to pen another book?

From Jazmin:

To Richard, for always being my most vocal and solid champion.

To my mom, for teaching me to cook scrambled eggs when I still needed a stool to reach the stovetop.

To Riley and Embry, for being my "why" and for teaching me to be a better human every day.

To my entire extended family of Flamands, Zepedas, and Blaises, you're all the best support section anyone could ask for.

To Scarlett, Jocelyn, and Chris, for pulling off a photo shoot on a moment's notice.

And to our Victory Belt team, Lance, Susan, Pam, Holly, Justin, Kat, and the many others who had a hand in making this book come together, your gentle pressure and guidance made this process enjoyable.

DIET AND ALLERGEN GUIDE

 DAIRY-FREE GLUTEN-FREE

 VEGETARIAN VEGAN

O = OPTION

RECIPE	PAGE	🥛	🌾	🥬	Ⓥ
Richie's Ranch Dressing	28		X	O	
Garlic & Mint Yogurt Sauce	30		X	X	
My Favorite Egg Dressing (Sauce Gribiche)	32	X	X	X	
Blais Béarnaise	34		X	X	
Miso Mustard	36	X	X		
Quick Pickles	38	X	X	X	X
Chimichurri	40	X	X		
Escabeche (Spicy Pickled Carrots)	42	X	X	X	X
Wild Blueberry Chia Jam	44	X	X	X	X
Cashew Cheese Spread	46	X	X	X	X
Sprouted Walnuts	48	X	X	X	X
Charred Vegetable Salsa	50	X	X	X	X
Vegetarian Demi-Glace	52	X	X	X	
Balsamic Glaze	54	X	X	X	O
Tomato & Watermelon Poke	60	X			
Gazpacho	62	X	X	X	X
Shakshouka with Chickpeas & Peppers	64	O	X	X	
Tomato Confit Toast with Cashew Cheese	66	X	O	X	O
THE Tomato with Yuzu & Shiso	68	X		X	X
Pizza & Sauce	70			X	
Spaghetti Pomodoro with Olives, Capers & Anchovies	72	X	O		
"Cincinnati-Style" Meatless Chili	74	X	O	X	O
Creamy Cauliflower & Coconut Soup	80	O	X	O	O
Cauliflower Fried Rice	82	X	O	X	
Cauliflower Nuggets with Buffalo Sauce & Quick Pickled Vegetables	84		X	X	
Cauliflower White Pizza with Cashew Cheese, Truffle Oil & Mushrooms	86	X	X	X	O
Jerk-Spiced Cauliflower Steaks	90	X	X	X	O
Roasted Whole Head of Cauliflower with Aromatics & Sultanas	92		X	X	
Cauli-Mac 'n' Cheese	94		O		
Easiest Potato Rosti	100	X	X	X	

RECIPE	PAGE	🍶	🌾	🥜	Ⓥ
Sweet Potato Hash Burritos with Eggs & Soy Chorizo	102		X	X	
Pommes Anna	104	O	X	X	
Baked Sweet Potato Fries with Garlic Mayo	106	X	X	X	
Potatostones (Potato Tostones)	108		X	X	
Thanksgiving-Style Baked Sweet Potatoes	110		X	O	
Mashed Rutabaga	112	O	X	X	O
A Simple Roasted Chicken with Vegetables from the Fridge	114	X	O		
A Nice Spinach Salad with Sprouted Walnuts & Dried Mulberries	122	O	X	X	O
Way Better Coleslaw	124		X	X	
Everyday Kale Salad with Avocado & Pine Nuts	126	X	X	X	X
Spinach Artichoke Dip	128	O	X	X	O
Caldo Verde (Green Soup)	130	X	X	O	O
Shaved Kale Salad with Coconut Cashew "Caesar" Dressing	132	O	X		
Broccoli Top "Pesto" with Kale & Whole-Wheat Spaghetti	134	O	O	O	O
Melting Cabbage with Good Butter, Pickling Spices & Dill	138		X	X	
Crispy Brussels Sprouts with Chili, Lime & Coconut Sugar	140	X	X		
Sautéed Spinach with Black Garlic & Lemon	142	X	X	X	X
Braised Holiday Greens	144	X	X	O	O
Parsnip Creamed Spinach	146	X	X	X	X
Herby Baked Salmon	148	X	X		
Jazmin's Green Smoothie	150	X	X	O	O
Chocolate Almond Smoothie	152		X	X	
Butternut Squash Soup	158	O	X	X	O
Zucchini Fritters with Parmesan	160		X	O	
Spaghetti Squash with the Simplest Tomato Sauce	162	X	X	X	X
Zucchini al Pastor with Yogurt	164		X	X	
Gluten-Free Pumpkin Bread	166	O	X	X	
Chocolate Squash Mousse	168		X	X	
Crunchy Carrot Slaw with Kale, Almonds, Apples & Raisins	174	X	X	X	
Carrot Coconut Soup with Cilantro & Lemongrass	176	X	X	O	
Grilled Carrots	178	O	X	O	
Chicken Shawarma & Spicy Carrot Hummus with Grilled Za'atar Naan	182	O			
Barbecued Carrots with Tomato, Coriander & Honey	186	X	X	X	
Lamb Braised Carrots with Dukkah & Yogurt	188		X	O	
Charred Carrot Hot Dogs	190	X	O	X	
Carrot Osso Buco with Polenta	192	X	X	O	
Gluten-Free Carrot Cake	196	O	X	X	
Porcini Omu-lette	204		X	X	

RECIPE	PAGE	🍷	🌾	🧈	Ⓥ
Shaved Button Mushroom Salad with Truffle Oil & Lemon	206	O	X	X	O
Cauliflower Crepes with Mushrooms & Prosciutto	208		X		
Mushroom Toast with Sherry & Goat Cheese	210			X	
Portobello Tartlettes with Baked Goat Cheese & Caramelized Onions	212	O	X	X	
Mushroom Risotto	214		X	O	
The 50/50 Mushroom Burger	216	X	X		
Mushroom Bolognese	218		O	O	
Roast Beast with Horseradish Ranch & Sherry-Glazed Mushrooms	220		X		
Creamy Mushrooms Glazed in Sherry	222		X	X	
Caponata Bruschetta	228	X		X	O
Baba Ghanoush	230		X	X	
Grilled Eggplant & Tomato Salad	232	O	X	X	
Eggplant & Chickpea Samosas	234	X		X	
Penne with Eggplant, Pesto, Chili & Feta	236		O	X	
Eggplant Braised in Sake, White Miso & Agave	238	X	X	X	X
Moussaka	240		X	O	
Eggplant Parmesan	242	O	X	O	
Banana Pancakes	248	O	O	X	
Buckwheat Pancakes with Kefir, Banana & Sprouted Walnuts	250			X	
Coconut Pancakes	252	O	X	X	
Petit Pois-camole (Frozen Pea Guacamole)	254	X	X	X	X
Chickpea "Tuna" Salad	256	X	X	X	O
Avocado Mac Salad	258		O	X	
Grilled Corn Salad with Cotija & Jalapeño	260		X	X	
Blistered Snap Peas with Feta & Mint	262		X	X	
Summer Vegetable Succotash	264	O	X	O	
Mulligatawny Stew	266	X	X		
Simple Chana Masala	268	X	X	X	
Baked Falafel	270		X	X	
Mango Sticky "Rice" Chia Pudding	272	X	X	X	X
Anytime Almond Biscuits	274		X	O	
THE Grain-Free Cookie	276	O	X	X	O

RECIPE INDEX

PANTRY

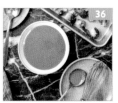

TOMATO

Tomato & Watermelon Poke

Gazpacho

Shakshouka with Chickpeas & Peppers

Tomato Confit Toast with Cashew Cheese

THE Tomato with Yuzu & Shiso

Pizza & Sauce

Spaghetti Pomodoro with Olives, Capers & Anchovies

"Cincinnati-Style" Meatless Chili

CAULIFLOWER

Creamy Cauliflower & Coconut Soup

Cauliflower Fried Rice

Cauliflower Nuggets with Buffalo Sauce & Quick Pickled Vegetables

Cauliflower White Pizza with Cashew Cheese, Truffle Oil & Mushrooms

Jerk-Spiced Cauliflower Steaks

Roasted Whole Head of Cauliflower with Aromatics & Sultanas

Cauli-Mac 'n' Cheese

POTATOES AND OTHER STARCHY THINGS

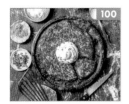

Easiest Potato Rosti

Sweet Potato Hash Burritos with Eggs & Soy Chorizo

Pommes Anna

Baked Sweet Potato Fries with Garlic Mayo

Potatostones (Potato Tostones)

Thanksgiving-Style Baked Sweet Potatoes

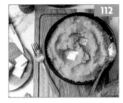

Mashed Rutabaga

A Simple Roasted Chicken with Vegetables from the Fridge

GREENS

A Nice Spinach Salad
with Sprouted Walnuts
& Dried Mulberries

Way Better Coleslaw

Everyday Kale Salad
with Avocado &
Pine Nuts

Spinach
Artichoke Dip

Caldo Verde
(Green Soup)

Shaved Kale Salad
with Coconut Cashew
"Caesar" Dressing

Broccoli Top "Pesto"
with Kale & Whole-
Wheat Spaghetti

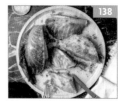

Melting Cabbage
with Good Butter,
Pickling Spices & Dill

Crispy Brussels Sprouts
with Chili, Lime &
Coconut Sugar

Sautéed Spinach with
Black Garlic & Lemon

Braised
Holiday Greens

Parsnip
Creamed Spinach

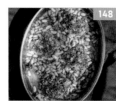

Herby Baked Salmon

Jazmin's
Green Smoothie

Chocolate Almond
Smoothie

SQUASH

Butternut Squash Soup

Zucchini Fritters with Parmesan

Spaghetti Squash with the Simplest Tomato Sauce

Zucchini al Pastor with Yogurt

Gluten-Free Pumpkin Bread

Chocolate Squash Mousse

CARROTS

Crunchy Carrot Slaw with Kale, Almonds, Apples & Raisins

Carrot Coconut Soup with Cilantro & Lemongrass

Grilled Carrots

Chicken Shawarma & Spicy Carrot Hummus with Grilled Za'atar Naan

Barbecued Carrots with Tomato, Coriander & Honey

Lamb Braised Carrots with Dukkah & Yogurt

Charred Carrot Hot Dogs

Carrot Osso Buco with Polenta

Gluten-Free Carrot Cake

MUSHROOMS

Porcini Omu-lette

Shaved Button Mushroom Salad with Truffle Oil & Lemon

Cauliflower Crepes with Mushrooms & Prosciutto

Mushroom Toast with Sherry & Goat Cheese

Portobello Tartlettes with Baked Goat Cheese & Caramelized Onions

Mushroom Risotto

The 50/50 Mushroom Burger

Mushroom Bolognese

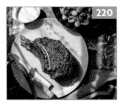
Roast Beast with Horseradish Ranch & Sherry-Glazed Mushrooms

Creamy Mushrooms Glazed in Sherry

EGGPLANT

Caponata Bruschetta

Baba Ghanoush

Grilled Eggplant & Tomato Salad

Eggplant & Chickpea Samosas

Penne with Eggplant, Pesto, Chili & Feta

Eggplant Braised in Sake, White Miso & Agave

Moussaka

Eggplant Parmesan

GRAINS, LEGUMES, AND EVERYTHING ELSE

Banana Pancakes

Buckwheat Pancakes with Kefir, Banana & Sprouted Walnuts

Coconut Pancakes

Petit Pois-camole (Frozen Pea Guacamole)

Chickpea "Tuna" Salad

Avocado Mac Salad

Grilled Corn Salad with Cotija & Jalapeño

Blistered Snap Peas with Feta & Mint

Summer Vegetable Succotash

Mulligatawny Stew

Simple Chana Masala

Baked Falafel

Mango Sticky "Rice" Chia Pudding

Anytime Almond Biscuits

THE Grain-Free Cookie

GENERAL INDEX

B